CARE SHARING
&
CARE HOMES
FOR OUR LOVED ONES

for whom every extra moment counts

by David Geraghty
a successful Rehab Stroke Patient

Michael Terence
Publishing

I want to dedicate this book to
THE TWO PILLARS IN MY LIFE,
*namely my sons, Daragh and Shane
and to Michelle & The Unknown Warrior.*

From Adult to Infant – in 90 Seconds!

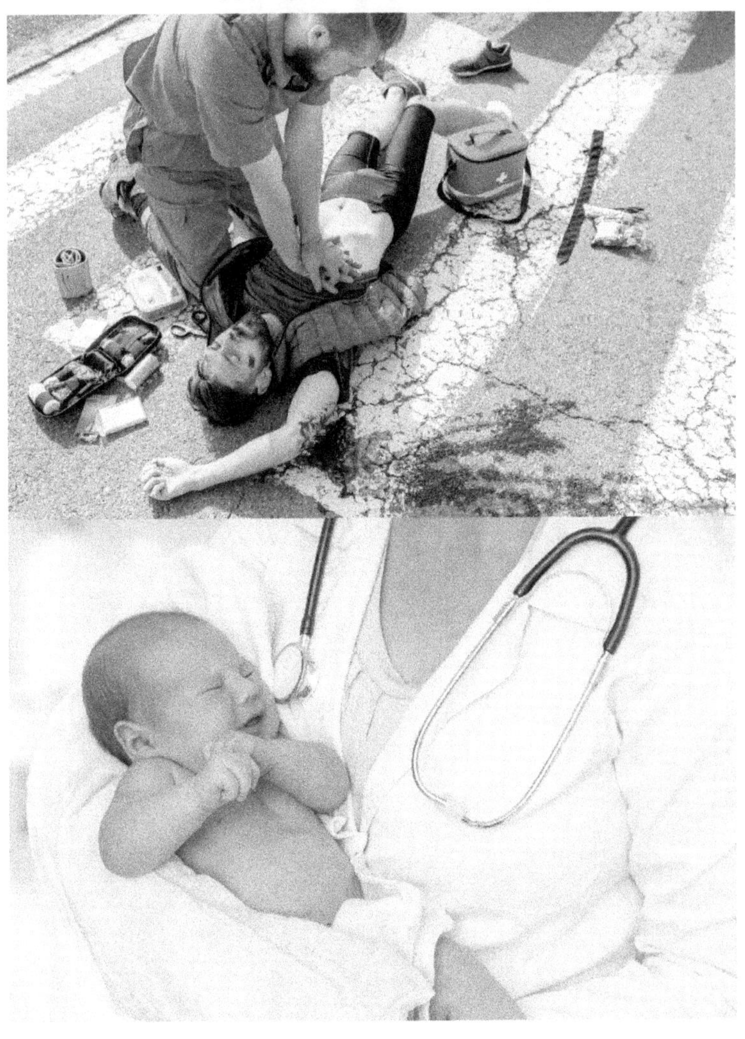

Contents

Foreword

Hi and welcome to my world! I am David. Now that you have picked this book off the shelf, maybe, like me, you are thinking that this scenario will never, ever, be for you. I was a serious naysayer. So, don't put it back on the shelf, as the knowledge within these pages may prolong and even save your life.

None of us are infallible, so we should always expect the unexpected as we will never know the second, the hour or the day when we may be afflicted by a stroke or any other sudden life-changing event. I was catapulted from being an athletic, intelligent adult to an infant in 90 seconds.

The knowledge contained in this book will be a positive addition to your reading collection for you, your family and your friends. I am a stroke survivor from Ireland. Some 3 years ago in 2018, as I am writing this in 2021, my current disposition was never envisaged nor that this would be how I would spend my retirement.

I am in my second care home to date and I can offer you some insight into these facilities. They are not end-of-life facilities, quite the opposite. They increase their residents' longevity, through quality care and attention. They are run and managed by skilled healthcare professionals. Here we have none of the daily stresses of normal life on the outside

I am very happy and content with my life here, as it is my best holiday to date. Time is our friend here, as we have no deadlines only appointments. I am grateful for my stroke, as it has been one of the most profound events of my life, second only to attending the births of my two sons.

Like most of you, I am living through Covid and hopefully, I shall live to see the end of the pandemic and return to the 'old normal'. I often refer to all my fellow residents as 'petals' because we are all the same, just different. Don't be apprehensive; it is the destiny of mankind to reside in a care home in a new normal, at some time in our future. We cannot stop the clock of ageing, infirmity or unexpected incidents. So, when it is your turn, embrace it. You will not regret it.

Look around you, they are developing care homes in every city, town and village. Across the whole world, this is our last stop-over en route to the next life!

I am now three years into this 'new normal' amidst the Covid pandemic, raging around our universe. Can I recommend life in a care home? As I have already extended my life by two years, from 70 to 72 and find myself included in my family's hopes and celebrations, which I and they would have missed out on, if my life span had not been extended, I can!

1

Who Am I?

I am David, a stroke-recovering gentleman from Ireland who missed out on "The Golden Hour." This is the first hour from the appearance of the symptoms of a stroke (F.A.S.T.) in which you have to reach a hospital if you are to benefit from clot-busting drugs and early medical diagnosis. Anything over this hour means a late diagnosis and the brain may be adversely affected. In my case, paralysis ensued, on my left side, leaving me disabled.

F.A.S.T. F = face drooping. A = arms dropping by your sides and feeling very heavy, as if you're holding a weight in each hand. S=slurred speech. T= time to call 999/112.

After being induced, I was told I would need full-time care 24/7/365 for the rest of my life. Being paralysed on my left side, my options were limited as I could not return home; my house was not suitable for me and I could not and still cannot afford full-time care. Once my physiotherapy recovery had plateaued while in hospital, the hospital's only concern was to have their bed back. A Flu epidemic was raging in our city and beds were needed urgently. So, they wanted me to move into a care home. With this request order hanging over me, my family and I had to figure out which particular care home? It's not a case of knocking on a care home door and walking in, as there is always a process and my family and I had to research the homes available to me.

My transition to our chosen care home was something of a novelty for me, having spent 14 months in hospital. My initial fears were will it be like an institution; a prison for instance or a mental home? I am happy to relate to you that none have been the case to date.

The most significant aspects turned out to be the teamwork between family members and me, as the patient, letting go, accepting and not resisting the inevitable. Most importantly, your family members are the ones who pick up the pieces you have left behind and put them back together again, so that you may exist and live. There is no 'I' or 'me' in 'team'.

Flower Petals

Someday, you will be a petal just like me and, in the pages ahead, I refer to all patients, whether they be in hospitals, mental institutions, elderly homes, care homes as petals. This is a term of endearment used globally, because like petals, regardless of our ailments, we are all the same, just different. We have no lines of demarcation and wear no ID labels. We are normal human beings encased within our own afflictions. We are also proud people with goals, hopes and aspirations! In our world hard things are put in our way, not to stop us but to call out to our courage and strength and the will to live for every extra moment that has been gifted to us. Care Homes are part of this gift, too.

Each petal begins life as a bud, with its own molecular make-up, as we have in our DNA. Each has its own colour and shape and no matter how many that bloom the world over, no two are exactly the same. Just like us, we are all different. We are all kinds of everything; remember Dana's winning Eurovision song in 1970?

The recent pandemic has really highlighted our vulnerability as your loved ones and is like an international banner across the world. There has never been such a public global outpouring and awareness for our welfare. Disability for us is not a brave struggle in the face of adversity, it is an ingenious way to live. We have to deal with it first thing every morning, when I and many like me, awake and see the wheelchair at the bedside. It can be like awakening from a nightmare, one for me which lasted 90 seconds and is a **Stark Reminder** of the day's struggles ahead. When we open our eyes to our world, it is always there to greet and remind us, each day with nowhere to hide. On reflection, I am not disabled by my disabilities but very thankful for the abilities that I have, more than I realise. At least I still have abilities.

My Doc, Joe. Blood and PSA Test

I am David, an Irish professional tour guide. I attended my Doc. Joe, for my annual Prostate Specific Antigen test, otherwise known as a PSA. This is a simple blood test, taken from your arm and not from your pouch, as some would have you believe. I do it each year to check for prostate cancer. You may be aware that most athletes worldwide grow beards and moustaches each autumn, while many remove them to support the issue and awareness of testicular cancer. Men are the world's worst patients. No men are immune to it. Don't be a member of team one, hung-low, have your PSA test done and don't lose your manhood and walk with a limp, off-balance.

I informed Joe of acute pains in my muscles, post-exercise (cycling). I assumed (wrongly) this was caused by lactic acid build-up. Doc Joe did not agree and told me to roll up my sleeve, he would do a blood test. When this returned from the lab, the results showed that there was no iron in my blood (none), consequently, my circulation (blood) was being starved of oxygen.as haemoglobin is the element (the courier) of our blood that transports Oxygen, throughout our bodies. Iron is a mineral that the body needs for growth and development. Your body uses iron to make haemoglobin, a protein in red blood cells that carries oxygen from the lungs to all parts of the body, and myoglobin, a protein that provides oxygen to muscles. Your body also needs iron to make some hormones. As a result, iron deficiency ANEMIA may leave you tired and short of breath and aching muscles, post-exercise.

He explained that the body uses iron to make haemoglobin - a protein in the red blood cells that collects and transports the iron which carries the oxygen in my circulation and which transfers to all organs, including my brain. So now we had a dilemma. How was I losing blood? Stools? Internal bleeding?

A **COLONOSCOPY** was called for, which is an investigation of my digestive tract and bowel Using a camera probe, carried out by a surgeon. This identified several polyps, like boils on the lining of my tracts which after a biopsy were deemed cancerous. I was released to go home after my procedure, Later that evening. While using the urinal at home, I heard a storm blowing up outside . When I opened the bathroom window, all I could see were white stars which I assumed was a snowstorm (a blizzard) however, it was all of the above was in my brain, not in the sky outside. Feeling unbalanced, I fell into a cast-iron bath, which I thought was a clump of snow, so I had no fear falling into it, then discovered I had no way of getting out of it as I had no power down my left side. Lying on my back like a beached Turtle on its back, on a beach I realized that I was powerless and helpless, as I struggled to get onto my knees, with no movement from my left-hand side, as I slipped and slid on the shower gel in the base of the bath, totally confused, disorientated, with snow and circles, tornadoes blurring my vision.

However, all of the above was in my brain, not in the sky outside. Feeling unbalanced, I fell into a cast-iron bath, which I thought was a clump of snow, so I had no fear falling into it.

Then I discovered that I had no way of getting out of it as I had no power down my left side and I was lying on my back like a beached turtle. As I struggled to get onto my knees, with no movement from my left, I slipped and slid on the shower gel in the base of the bath, totally confused and disorientated, with snow circles and tornadoes blurring my vision.

Realising that I was powerless and helpless, I covered my upper torso with shower gel using my right hand and slid out of the bath, like a seal off a ledge and somehow crawled back to my room. My greatest fear in those moments was what if there was a fire coming up the stairs? I was very frightened!

Some hours later, I managed to raise the alarm via my cell phone. When the paramedics, Sarah and Steven from Clonbur Rescue Services arrived, they found me stark naked, wet and in an advanced state of **HYPOTHERMIA**, no pain sensation at all, just silence. They duly took control and immediately wrapped me up like a Christmas cracker in thermal silver blankets. I was still unaware of the gravity of my condition. However, Sarah and Steven left me in no doubt and warned me not to give in to sleep, otherwise, it would be a permanent one. Stay awake I did, as we made our way to the hospital.

This really scared me. I chatted with the driver and the paramedics all the way to the hospital, pointing out well-known venues along the route through the side window of the ambulance, as a form of "association awareness". I felt very tired but sleep was not an option for me, which kept me very focussed and no doubt played a very important role in my future recovery. To this day, Association is my first task every morning as it is the key to my daily safety; the areas surrounding our bedsides can be like minefields with all the clutter we humans gather up.

We duly arrived at University Hospital Galway, (UHG) Ireland and I noticed a lot of men wearing high-viz vests. Now very aware and apprehensive, I enquired if we were at the cuckoo's nest, aka the madhouse and I cursed the driver for getting lost!

Within minutes, the rear doors opened and I was enveloped in a sea of medics in white uniforms and taken for a Cat-Scan on my brain and was duly induced and diagnosed.

Brain Inducement or Reversible Coma is an effective medical procedure used in cases of extreme trauma, such as Stroke. This shutting down of brain function allows the brain time to heal, without the body performing radical triage by turning off blood flow to damaged sections. This is a form of Anaesthesia. (See Scientific American).

So, folks, many hours later, as I emerged from my coma, feeling somewhat confused, groggy and more, I realised that I was wearing some foreign object between my legs. So, I beckoned to my Ward Nurse, Kate, a fiery redhead from Connemara. She came to my bedside and I pointed to the diaper.

"What's this all about?" I enquired.

"You have been comatose for 12 hours, so we didn't want you peeing in your jocks and getting a rash on your groin," she replied.

"So, I am like a newborn, then?"

"Bang on," she replied.

"Did I get a smack on my arse?"

"No, Dave," she replied. "That only happens in the movies!"

Agreat start to a **NEW NORMAL LIFE** and a return to my old life of **Assisted Living**, as a new-born 69 years ago, where and when my life's journey began at my first birth!

2

Hospital Life at UHG and Merlin Park

Assisted Living. Life in a Wheelchair

Still groggy, I noticed I was surrounded by beds, with males requesting to have their diapers changed and asking was it ok for them to do their poos in them? Hearing this, I felt convinced I was in the cuckoo's nest. It got worse. One of the nurses on the ward shouted to Kate:

"Kate, Dave has no Pinky!"

No penis? OMG! What's THIS that all about? I had to have a peep and fumbled under the blankets; it was still there, intact. Phew! Is this a hospital or an abattoir? I thought and of course, I couldn't go anywhere. Then the whole ward cracked up with everyone in hysterics! The other lads shouting, did they take your bottle brush as well? **MY PECKER** found; everyone **PERKED UP!**

Later I learnt that a "pinky" is nurses' terminology for an absorption blanket.

That night, I was transferred to Merlin Park, a sister hospital of UHG, which dealt with most stroke patients on arrival at A&E. Later that morning, my family visited me and of course, this had become their tragedy too. I felt privileged to have them at my bedside but guilty for all the upset I had caused. One of them even had to fly in at short notice from London.

When they were informed of my tragic event the previous evening, they were told that I had 72 hours left to live. Now, I am one of only 10% who survives their first stroke. I was classified as an acute patient, with an acquired brain injury. This represented the beginning of my battle with **INCONTINENCE**. I was already familiar with the consequences of it from overseas tourists, whom I had driven all over Ireland. Acute patients can't navigate, nor walk the hospital wards or corridors to make it to the bathroom in a hurry, therefore diapers were the easy option for the hospital staff, for safety reasons. So, I was determined not to give in to this easy option, bearing in mind the issues it creates with social constraints, social interaction, with family, friends, using taxis, foreign travel, restaurants, etc., etc.

Daily Life in Hospital

Physiotherapy

Each morning began with the Physiotherapy team at 8.30 am for one hour in the Physio Room. This 'Room of Hope,

Pain and Expectation' for me and many like me, was our daily routine from Monday to Friday. The patience and dedication of Joan and her team, Niamh and Liam, was remarkable, with their persistence, patience and willpower to encourage us to succeed at our tasks. And if we did fall or fail, they would pick us up again, with a pat on the back and a smile, whispering: "We will try it again and be better tomorrow!"

These are Neuro Therapists, who are Human Electricians, as they try to reconnect or re-wire the old neural pathways and stimulate our central nervous system, via repetitive exercises on the affected areas of our bodies. With a stroke, the trauma of it is so dramatic, it's like a fuse board exploding, like an electrical storm.

I became a Google junkie, researching the route to the Silver Bullet, which I led myself to believe was Technology or Electrical Stimulation but Joan, a true Kerry lass, was having none of it. And there was no venting with Joan, just common sense on my part. Dave, keep your mouth shut!

Now, this was to be my initiation into the beginning of my new life, my New Normal of Assisted Living. Still considered High Risk, I was placed in a male acute ward, mostly occupied by Stroke patients. Each of us looked similar, being bed-bound and very ill. The standard message to all of us by the Nursing and Medical staff was that all strokes differ and no two are the same. This was to alleviate the anxiety of those of us, who were paralysed when we would see someone such as a bedside neighbour getting out of bed and going walkabout. That was always upsetting.

Our days were dominated by physiotherapy. We, acute patients, did not really mingle or were socially active, due to a constant stream of visitors throughout the day. I spent most of my time on the internet, looking for the Silver Bullet, that might reverse my paralysis, of which there were two chances: slim or none at all! I spent a lot of time alone. As my family lived six hours away from the hospital.

Evenings were spent behind the curtains in my cubicle, listening to all the visitors (not mine) and their myriads of questions, all of which were the same. Top of the discussions were the Physiotherapists and Physiotherapy; everyone whispering to the patients, that you have to work hard at your daily Physio. Most patients hated it and did not need this daily reminder.

It shocked me how revered the Therapists were, even more so than the Surgeons who had just replaced your hips. They knew it and soaked up the adulation, which is why they have **BIG SMILES**. Stroke, acute patients with paralysis do require Neuro Physiotherapy, with Neuro-qualified Therapists, who are very scarce.

Therapists will not give up on you, so it is now a partnership of sorts, a case of patience vs progress, self-belief and willpower. Most Therapists rarely complete a patient's rehab, as they neither have the time nor the resources to see it to the end. When mine finished up with me, I got him a new job selling and fitting Mollii suits, which are similar to wet suits packed with electrodes for Electrical Stimulation. I was the first patient to try this in Ireland and it is very impressive (see the section *Back from The Brink*).

Medical Team

After physio, it was back to the ward to meet the medical team assigned to me, led by Dr Tom Walsh. His team were like The World Foreign Legion, an eclectic mix of mostly young female doctors, drawn from all four corners of the world, all of whom wore stilettos. I would hear them coming down the marble corridors led by Professor Robinson - no wilting violet, this is Real Woman -with a wall of noise: clickity-clack, clickity-clack, clickity-clack, like the old steam train on tracks. They were all beautiful and dressed very stylishly to perk us up as if they had been coming home from a nightclub. Then the smiles, salutations, questions, interrogation, nods and prods, the whispering in a language all their own and of course the smiles and more oriental salutations! Then the Heel Brigade were gone for another day. Until Tomorrow.

The Lighter Moments

In any location, there are characters and we had ours. Mike de Hoist, a very big man and the head honcho of the Daily Diaper Brigade to raise the butts of the diaper patients from their beds, by their heels for their daily inspection and pampering. No mechanical hoists needed when Mike, a human hoist, was around. Then on to the shower room, "The Moon Room" for Under the Bonnet Cleansing and more. Mike would instruct:

"Drop your togs and lean against the rail, touch your toes and let your butt see the moon and we will have a "bit of crack." Once we did as he said, he continued: "Let me clean your Grand Canyon."

We'd stay bent over and he produced a nylon sweeping brush doing the business and he would howl with laughter, saying:

"Wasn't that great crack!"

Mind you it was a pleasant experience, slightly ticklish on the sphincter port-hole! Then he would hose us all with cold water, while he howled with laughter again and we EFFED him forever more, as he herded us back to our wards. We never found out if he used the same sweeping brush to clean all his Grand Canyons.

A new care assistant came into the ward on a Sunday morning and pointed at me:

"YOU! out of that bed; you are for a shower."

I didn't refuse, because I figured this one was a rough diamond and so, off we went with me in the mobile shower chair. Once in the shower room, she got down to business and handed me some shower gel and started hosing me from head to toe.

"Now, clean under the bonnet yourself," she instructed.

"It's itchy there," I replied and asked if she had any Canesten thrush cream?

Well, that got her blood boiling. She glared and handed me the shower hose, saying:

"Rinse the itch, yourself."

Instead, I drenched her from head to toe and I can't repeat the blue language that erupted from her lips. Furious, she grabbed the hose from me, threw a few towels at me and started wheeling me back to the ward, whilst hitting me on the head with a clean diaper, shouting:

"You fucker, you fucker, may you Effin' twitch all day and night with the ITCH, you fucker!"

I was in convulsions of laughter. It was the best tonic I had in there for 14 months, better than all the medication. I am in convulsions now at the memory of it as I type this. I never did get the Thrush cream. That bird flew off with a beak full of Fuckers - and that was mild - and never flew back, definitely not a homing pigeon, and nobody ever knew what occurred.

That laugh did more for me than any medication. No more shower offers from her, only dirty looks. Amidst all the daily commotion, were the nurses, healthcare Angels, cleaners, kitchen staff and Wee Mary, our receptionist who was always kitted out for a cocktail party in stilettoes. Collectively they all added to the quality of my daily life.

We clashed too from time to time, as Radic and Joan, "Blondie" will agree but we parted on good terms.

The Sout/Porter Theory

I did leave the medical team with a conundrum: the stout/porter theory. I outlined to the team that the colonoscopy never fully explained my blood loss and I never did get a definitive answer as to how I was losing blood. So, I gave them my own theory. Because I consumed a lot of stout/porter, the odd time I might look into the toilet bowl after doing a 'number two', I would notice that the excrement could look somewhat black, without the creamy head, and that it would be impossible to discern if there were any traces of blood there. The team are still out whispering and nodding. I guess as I haven't heard a clickity-clack since; maybe the shoes are with the cobbler? Or in the pawn shop, given their jnr. Doctor hospital salaries?

Over the next few weeks, within my acute ward, similar acute patients were arriving and others departing, six of them in basket-woven coffins; scary is not even close! While there, I survived being electrocuted, having picked up a live electric shaver I had dropped on the floor. At this time, I was not very connected with my God, so I decided to re-connect, otherwise, I could have found myself underground, giving 'Oul Ned, (the devil) a hand shovelling coal and having my eyebrows singed.

Reconnecting has been the best decision of my life to date. I had my bowel cancer op with a positive outcome a short time later. I was also diagnosed with Sleep Apnea. Having stopped breathing 114 times in one night, I was destined to pass away peacefully throughout the night or daytime but the nursing staff had kept a vigil on me overnight as Stroke patients are known to be susceptible to Sleep Apnea. When my family were informed, they said I did this all the time while at home, they just didn't know what it was. So, keep an eye on each other at home. I now have to wear an air mask every night.

I promised to find a way of giving back to others, who may find themselves enduring a similar tragedy to mine and hopefully find some snippet in this book, that will offer them some solace on their journey.

I felt I was a Nobody but then I realised everyone is Someone and needs a body. So, now I am a perfect Somebody, after all my trauma, scans and x-rays, medical poking and prodding! All of my organs functioned normally, including my reproductive region, with many questions, light-hearted ones from friends, about the nether region: is it up? or down? What is the same for all, is that all major organs function normally and the male genitals, which aroused (excuse the pun) much curiosity about my erectile malfunction or not? My reply was: it's never been longer or stronger!

The penis is now the subject of the early-morning scourge of PRIAPISM - go to google quickly and beat the queue - in virile males. So, how does one get rid of the nuisance? I can hear you all shouting: "Jerk it!" but that's not practical in a ward of ten other patients. The cure, not yet licensed, is just to drink lots of water and urinate. No patent required, just patience. Job done!

Thanks to The Pogue Mahone Research Institute in Galway for their loyal dedication to the **Male Organ of DELIGHT** for many! Do it before the nurses roll back the blankets because man is the only animal that blushes. Now, it's on to the unexpected phase of my new extended life. Isn't it great we can still have a broom handle to raise the flag of hope and glory!

3

Stroke

I really struggled with the sheer oblivion of my Stroke and could never find a definition for it, that would give me some meaning and solace. Until that is, I awoke this morning 4 years later, when I had that eureka moment, which explained it all to me in one fleeting thought, that oblivion is the darkest and the blackest of any blackness imaginable. Blacker than black is hard to imagine, especially in the cul-de-sacs and blind alleyways of my mind, with not a ray of light to be seen from any source; could anyone imagine Guinness to be any blacker than it is? Until I began to mix with those in my stroke support group (www.croi.ie) and see with my own eyes, those who had travelled a similar journey as mine to that first day with them and more to follow and witness with my own eyes, their progress, attitude, positivity and willingness to reach out to their fellow victims.

I was no longer a Nobody encased within a **HOLLOW** shell but was now Someone again, a 'Petal', ready to bloom again, and **Still Blooming** 4 years later. Attending these get-togethers lets you see how others overcome their affliction and share with you their way of dealing with it. I tried to get an explanation for the word stroke in the

Oxford dictionary but all I could get was 'a Lash' - and the **ONE** I got was enough! So, I made up my own: S= stress; T=tolerance for all of the above; R=the relationships it fragmented; O=oblivion; K=kinetics/no walking etc; E=empathy - enough of that. All that=stroke!

Today, I am happy to relate to you, that I found the **RAY** of light and the **PETAL** is blooming **Brighter** as I exit the **Darkness** and **Oblivion** to a **Brighter** future, having found **THE LIGHT!** Go to your stroke support group and share with others. Do it today, don't delay.

Strokes. All of Which Are Silent

There are 3 tragedies at play here:

1. The Victim
2. The Family
3. The Friends

For many of us, this is our second journey, from Foetus to Infant to this **New Normal** of 2021. Let us compare:

Stroke: Adult to Infant in 90seconds. So, let us talk about Stroke and its related tragedies;

Adult	Infant	Adult
Hunger	Howls/kicks	Rings a bell
Thirst	a/a	a/a
Diaper dump	a/a	a/a
TLC	a/a	Cell phone
Fart damage	Giggles, pisses in your eye	Blushes

How do strokes occur? What is a stroke?

Adult to Infant in 90seconds, a Stroke is silent, with no indication of pain in advance of its occurrence. It is not in front of you, nor to either side of you or behind you, it is **within** you! When the blood supply to parts of your brain is interrupted, depriving the brain tissue of oxygen and nutrients, causing the brain cells or neurons to die in minutes and which cannot be replaced. In my case, a weak artery wall imploded with a subsequent bleed which would normally be fatal.

Some Helpful Hints
- just in case, for those susceptible to a stroke or mini-strokes who may be at home

If you are home alone, always keep some lights on. No one is immune to having a stroke; beware, if you are late 40s, 50s and so on. Stay alert, steady yourself, draw in deep, sharp breaths and exhale slowly. Help will always arrive. Stay focused; ensure the floor space around you is clear of obstacles before you move to get to a phone; practise the manoeuvre with a family member.

It's like a game of What if? with a family member. Because we never know when it could happen. I had 3 mini-strokes and the keyword for every stroke is: F.A.S.T. F = face drooping. A = arms dropping by your sides and feeling very heavy, as if you're holding a weight in each hand. S=slurred speech. T= time to call999/112.

No two strokes are the same regarding their outcome. If you live alone, get an Alarm Necklace. Just don't panic, because that will do nothing for you, except be a nuisance and who needs that at a time like this?

Now that you have read the above facts, practice What If? And try to live a healthy lifestyle which will be a whole lot easier than having to deal with an outcome that is non-reversible and has no vaccine.

With this request hanging over me, my family and I had to figure out which particular care home? It's not a case of knocking on the door and walking in, there is always a process and we had to research the homes available to me in my area.

My transition to our chosen care home was something of a novelty for me, having spent 14 months in hospital. My initial fears were will it be like an institution; a prison for instance or a mental home? I am happy to relate to you that to date neither has been the case. The most significant aspects turned out to be teamwork between family members and me, as the patient, letting go and accepting and not resisting the inevitable.

Most importantly, your family members are the ones who pick up the pieces you have left behind and put them back together again, so that you may exist and live.

Stroke Statistics

Ireland: each year, approximately 10,000 Irish people have a stroke and around 2,000 die; more deaths than breast cancer, prostate cancer and bowel cancer combined.

In the UK, there are more than 100,000 strokes each year. That is around one stroke every five minutes. There are over 1.2 million stroke survivors in the UK. Every two seconds, someone in the world will have a stroke.

In the USA, in 2018, 1 in every 6 deaths from cardiovascular disease was due to stroke. Someone in the United States has a stroke every 40 seconds. Every 4 minutes, someone dies of a stroke. Every year, more than 795,000 people in the United States have a stroke.

Globally, according to the World Health Organisation, 15 million people suffer strokes worldwide each year. Of these, 5 million die and another 5 million are permanently disabled. High blood pressure contributes to more than

12.7 million strokes worldwide. Europe averages approximately 650,000 stroke deaths each year.

Flint Rehabilitation Devices
- warning signs and symptoms of ruptured aortic aneurysms.

www.flintrehab.com

The danger of aortic aneurysms is there are no warning signs and symptoms to suggest that the disease develops. When symptoms present, it indicates the ruptures from the innermost layer to the middle layer and eventually to the outermost layer, which attaches the vessel to the surrounding tissue. The ruptured aortic aneurysms cause irregular blood circulation.

21 Useful Stroke Exercises www.flintrehab.com
- to Improve Mobility and Function at Home

Enquiries to: dave.gero@gmail.com

DVDs are available.

Stroke Support Meetings and Webinars

These are sources of great interaction for new stroke victims, where the new ones and not so new - the centurions - discuss the challenges they have to endure on a daily basis. At these meetings, we all speak openly about ourselves and exchange ideas on our solutions.

On our committee at www.croi.ie, we have two golden oldies, him and her, Monica and John, also known as The Golden Couple. They offered the most beneficial advice of all to date, which is **team work** between the victim and their family and vice-versa. We all know that there is no cure, unlike the current pandemic! If only we could have a jab! That is unlikely, so we just have to make do with our lot and for our loved ones to put up with us. Right now, the best friends we have are hope, technology, not medication and regardless of what country you live in, you will find a local Stroke Support Group.

Never let it get the better of you because you are stronger than it. So, it left you disabled, now be thankful for the abilities and choices that you still retain. Hard things are put in our way, not to stop us, but to call out our courage and strength. Our disability is not a brave struggle or courage in the face of adversity, disability is an art and an ingenious way to live. You are not disabled by the disabilities you have; you are enabled by the abilities you have. Stroke may have nullified some of our abilities but it has never nullified the word hope! It's in our natural DNA. Here is a good definition of it:

HOPE is a feeling of the wanting of a particular thing to happen and the aspiration to succeed through dedication, determination and skill and a yearning to overcome each setback along the way, plus the blinding ambition to reach the pinnacle of your chosen path and dream to make the world sit up and take notice and hope that we can return to our families and leave a legacy! Amen.

New-born babies are true hopers. As soon as they are laid down in their cots, the first thing they do is to make eye contact, a connection. Lying on their backs, they soon begin to raise up both arms, yearning for a teat or some food and affection. They will kick, howl, yell and scream until they get the attention they crave and they will never, ever give up. Neither should we. Stroke can leave a lot of broken bodies in its wake but it has never managed to break the spirit of hope, never! Hope stands for hang on, persist! (Ho-pe.)

There are many new, unexpected daily challenges such as learning how to swallow again. With metal chains up my nose and down the back of my throat, it was pure torture, hell. Ugh, I had to be weaned onto solid foods, with thickener in all my fluids, before leaving hospital. I was subjected to daily scans and x-rays of all my body organs, which alarmed me no end and I accused my medical team of looking for trouble! Each morning, I would hear the wooden wheelchair, like a kitchen chair, a gurney, with tiny wheels, squeaking as Tom, who looked like the Grim Reaper, pushed it down the corridor and into my ward. It was like a scene out of death row with no manacles.

Tom would look at me and I would ask what? Where? "Liver today," was the reply! He had a menu card of procedures and I would look back with dismay, as I did drink a lot of alcohol. I was really scared that day. The medical team did explain to me, that following stroke and the trauma my body and organs had endured, may have scarred them resulting in lesions or lacerations on my organs. Phew! I got the All Clear. These collections by Tom went on daily for weeks.

No Left Arm/Hand Function

This disability turned out to be far worse than I ever envisaged. Before this tragedy, I rarely gave it a second thought. As a daily utility appendage, it was always just there, where it was supposed to be. It's almost a living nightmare without it, even though I am right-handed. My Occupational Therapist never supported me in relation to physio for my left arm, even refusing me permission to engage my own therapist for remedial therapy for my hand and fingers. Mind you, she did suggest writing an essay on living without it, so here are some of the downsides experienced:

1. Can't cut my nails on my right hand.

2. Can't tie my laces.

3 Can't drive, change gears, steer.

4.Can't hold a Smartphone.

5. Can't propel the left wheel on my wheelchair.

6.Can't use gardening tools.

7 Can't play field sports.

8.Can't ride a bike and a lot more?

9.Can't give anyone a real hug or embrace.

This is my greatest and most annoying daily challenge.

Venting

I never knew much about this subject. I had an issue with the CEO of Croi, Neil Johnson, a man I had never met but felt I needed to give him a piece of my mind over their services. It was the full-on, Alex Fergusson hair drier – not a Dyson one - on full power, by email. Neil wrote back and thanked me for venting and that it was a positive thing to do.

Little did I know that the subject would arise again. One evening, I had an issue about something and I began to rant at the two senior nurses on duty and that my current doctor, Professor Shaun O'Keefe, who was very posh, was nothing but a QUACK!

Well, all hell broke loose; the nurses demanded an immediate apology and how dare I insult one of their colleagues. I refused and said I would apologise to him personally. For several days after this episode, I awaited the professor's morning arrival with nervous anticipation.

One morning, as he arrived, I beckoned to him.

"Prof, I owe you an apology."

I related to him the incident with the nurses.

"And I called you a QUACK of the highest order!"

I can honestly say that he 'quacked up laughing'! But when he did regain his self-control, he came over to me, took my hand and said that my apology was accepted and that he had been called worse! And we both had a good chuckle. He did advise me that it is good to vent from time to time as it gets rid of all that toxic energy and frustrations within us humans.

Counselling

Listen to the Niall Breslin podcast "Where is my mind?" and let us all have a conversation about nothing in particular.

Counselling is a subject that has been suggested to me on many occasions but being a naysayer, I always declined until I spoke with Martina, a Stroke Support leader with the Irish Heart Foundation. When I was doing research on Stroke and during our chat, she raised the topic of counselling and had I ever considered it? By the end of the conversation, I had agreed to give it a trial.

Martina was a true colleen, a charmer and so the following Wednesday at 10.30 am as had been arranged, a lady called Carol phoned me and this continued for many weeks. There were no set topics for each call; it was very much off the cuff. The conversations were never invasive or uncomfortable in any way, just very casual and I was always looking forward to the next time we would speak again.

As I alluded to earlier, there was a time when I felt that I was a nobody. I was very reluctant to lean on my two sons, as they needed to have their own space, as it is their tragedy also and I occupy a lot of their space anyhow. Family conversations can turn very sour with the wrong word or comment. The definite 'No' words to overuse are 'I' and 'me' and this is why my chats with Carol were so refreshing, as there were never any pot holes to trip over or a need to watch my P's and Q's and they all had a **Peaceful and Enlightening** conclusion as if **CAROL** has flicked a switch!

Now, this lady was and still is a complete stranger to me, who has my cell phone number but I am not permitted to have hers. However, if I need her, I can call Martina.

So, yes, I do recommend counselling, because it is good to talk and to off-load a little, without ranting or venting but if I wanted to, I could; there were no barriers: "just be yourself, Dave." I always felt very calm and confident and that I was somebody again, having got lost somewhere in **my re-birth**. There were never any recommendations, that I do A.B.C, or D, only: "We will chat next week." And **NEVER RANT** at your family, as the letter 'I' is not in Team and avoid the word 'Me'.

To sum it up, it was just good to talk to a stranger, for someone to shine a light on something lurking in my mind that was having a negative effect on me and which I was unaware of, like having a boil or a pimple on the back of your neck, that you cannot see and is annoying you and different from family, whom my tragedy affects on a daily basis. So, it's respectful, not to lean on them too much, as they need their space, even though we fill most of their space and we are not aware of it, or we choose not to, which would be very selfish. Lest we forget, our families have picked up the pieces we have left behind and put them back together again, so that we may exist and live! Imagine what they think when they see your number lighting up their phone: Oh-Oh, what's this going to be all about, another 'I or me' conversation?

Every Wednesday, a group of us Stroke patients, male and female, would meet up with our Occupational Therapist in the hospital where we would discuss our current feelings, which you must never trust as they keep changing. One lady in the group informed us that prior to her stroke, she had had cancer in her blood but was now free of it.

The three main types of blood cancer are leukaemia, lymphoma and myeloma. Leukaemia is a cancer that originates in the blood and bone marrow. It occurs when the body creates too many abnormal white blood cells and interferes with the bone marrow's ability to make red blood cells and platelets.

This lady prayed to her God day and night to return the leukaemia to her and remove the Stroke.

Avoid the anxiety of expectation, as progress is often very slow which can put a dent in your self-belief. Slow progress is better than no progress; you are only ever lost if you give up on yourself and all of those supporting your efforts.

Often my own **SILENCE** means I am tired of fighting and now that there is nothing left to fight for, **NO SILVER BULLET**. My silence means I am tired of expressing my feelings to you. But now I do not have the energy to explain these anymore, which means that I have adapted to the changes in my life and I don't want to be complaining anymore. My silence now indicates that I am on a 'healing' process and I am trying to forget everything, I ever wanted from you, except for my own version.

The difference between a successful person and others is not the lack of knowledge or a lack of strength but a lack of willpower, as there will be time for you to fledge and fly!

My Own Reflections 4 Years On

This morning 26/02/21, as I reflect on stroke and what it meant to me all those years ago. Back then in 2018, I searched the Oxford dictionary and others, looking for the meaning of it. To this day, I have never found one, except my own: the S - the T - the R - the O - the K - the E - equal STROKE.

S = Stress, dealing with my daily disabilities and
    challenges.

T = Tolerance, putting up with all of the above and
    it being non-reversible.

R = Relationships that it has fragmented. I learned
    that different family members deal with
    Tragedy very differently.

O = Oblivion. non-reversible and being stuck here
    – including my family - as if in quicksand,
    sinking and sinking and suffocating and no
    sign of a rescue party coming to pull us out! I
    might turn up on a golf course in a bunker.

K = Kinetics; no walking anymore. Your
    body also needs iron to make some hormones.
    As a result, iron deficiency anaemia may leave
    you tired and short of breath and with aching
    muscles, post-exercise.

E = Empathy, which we can do without as it only
    revives the nightmare that it is.

Time - not included - and which has been extended to my life, with special thanks to 'The Stiletto Brigade'. **SUMMING UP**, initially, I believed I had **DRAWN** the **SHORT STRAW**, but I ended up with **THE LONG ONE**, i.e. **MORE TIME!**

As this is **MY 2ND BIRTH**, mankind is very different to what I knew it to be before my event. Mankind is now completely **DIGITISED** and boring, all walking about with tv screens on their person and not a good channel on any of them.

The Mollii Suit

Regarding the fact that your body also needs iron to make some hormones. As a result, iron deficiency anaemia may leave you tired and short of breath and aching muscles, post-exercise: I tried the Mollii Suit and it is very impressive.

The Suit's soft Jacket and Trousers deliver a gentle sensory-level electro-stimulation to muscle groups programmed to each person's needs.

- Adjusting muscle activity and tone

- Preparing the body for therapy

- Regular use enhances neuroplasticity

- For adults and children from 3 years old

- Free Individual assessments

- Rental and purchase options

- Easy to use

For conditions including
- Cerebral Palsy

- Multiple Sclerosis

- Brain and Spinal Cord Injury

- Stroke

- Other neurological and movement disorders

- Chronic pain, Fibromyalgia etc.

I did try this out and the electrical stimulation does work very well. These suits may be rented on a monthly basis and fitted under supervision. Wonderful results with children and Spasticity.

Call +44 1730 269000 or Mollii@remotion.co.uk
Richard Walsh Myles. Mention David in Ireland.
www.mollii.com

4
Snapshots

For all who like me are cocooning on a regular basis, doing a snapshot of your daily life is very rewarding and uplifting at a glance. I will outline "all" below.

I am David, a recovering stroke patient for 2.9 years now, who has been cocooning all that time in hospital and nursing homes. So, I have had to find ways of stimulation, to have a smile on my face morning and night-time. I found the snapshot to be my stimulus! So, let me set it out for you and how to use it.

We normally associate a snapshot with a photo, a negative, a polaroid. It is none of these, it is you being your own lens and taking in all the events that occur in your day. Firstly, you need to be **ALERT** and tuned into your day. So, get an A4 pad, a ring binder with dividers, take a round plate or saucer and place it upside down on your A4 page. Then with a pen, trace the outline onto the paper. Use it like a clock face and mark points on it defining your "To do" list for the day, at specific times. Write your name in the centre of the circle, as you are the most important notation on this chart!

As your day progresses, place a tick beside jobs done and add to your circle, incoming calls from family and friends and so on. At the close of your day, analyse the positives on your chart and fill in a new one with the day's date, with a little personal summary at the end of the page. Was it a good day? Did it bring a smile? Then one last look, smile and prepare the next one for the following day. File it away in your ring binder. Do this for each day.

At end of the week, read through all your charts for the week and do a summary chart for the whole week, from your daily charts. Just take one glance at your snapshot; just one glance and there is your whole day!

1.   You will be amazed at how much you have achieved. At a glance!

2.   How busy you were and can be.

3.   You will have that fulfilled feeling!

4.   You will feel organised and mentally astute!

5.   This can be a journey that can be the key to open the door of Darkness into Light. The diagram below was posted on the CROI website: www.croi.ie for World International Stroke Day 29/10/2021.

- David

Sample below.

CALLS IN:

THE DAY & DATE:

YOUR NAME E-MAILS IN;

CALLS OUT:

YOUR VISITORS TODAY?

E-MAILS SENT:

SUMMARY OF YOUR DAY?

PREPARE TOMORROWS CHART.

Ask a family member to copy this and print off a batch for you and provide you with a clipboard and a ring binder.

5
Wheelchair Life

Rescue Bag + Poo-Bag

My wheelchair, a self-propelled one, when presented to me by my Physio team, was concrete affirmation that walking again normally was not for me. First came the fitting measurements and the cushion suitability. I thought I must be getting a Rolls Royce, with all the fuss. Trying to get used to it initially, I thought driving a bus would be a whole lot easier and I only have one arm to help propel me. This is another new adjustment for me, to manage with one arm and hand.

I could now travel the corridors and not being so bed-bound any more was a very welcome relief, mentally, as I now had some means of being independent. I was also able to venture out socially with family and friends, whereas up to this time, all I could envisage were dead-ends, cul-de-sacs and oblivion and feeling like I was a nobody.

The world of old was opening up again to me, which offered and still does offer a lot of solace to this day. A big thank you to the inventor of the wheel, Marcus Pollio. I declined a power chair, as in my current state I could do with burning some calories with my own effort, rather than becoming reliant again and giving up my new found independence.

I feel real again, accepted and not shunned on the outside by society. I felt I was a nobody but then I realised everyone is someone and needs a body. So, now I am a perfect somebody, after all my trauma, scans, x-rays and medical poking and prodding.

So, on to the unexpected phase of my new extended life, the Wheelchair. Regarding my transition and adaptation to life in a wheelchair, the first issue I discovered, concerned social interaction. But first, I have a question for you, the reader: When you look at someone in a wheelchair, do you assume that the individual in it is there as a result of some tragedy? I never looked at it that way myself, so I just had to learn fast and be analytic in advance of any pending social interaction, such as family visits and venturing out and about by myself. So, I created a list of Doos and Dont's for myself.

The Doos

Prepare well, such as having done your number Ones and Twos toilet and ablutions before leaving, in the safety of your hospital or care home. Ensure your mobile phone is fully charged. Phone and book a wheelchair taxi and ask how much the fare will be, which you can have ready; one thing less to worry about while in transit to your destination. Have a Care Assistant with you. If not, ensure that the phone number of your facility is in your phone, in case of emergency. Check with your nurse before you leave the facility. Have your home code sellotaped to your phone, in case you get lost.

Prepare a travel bag, in fact, a 'Rescue Bag', containing rubber gloves, a face towel, a few J-cloths, 3 face cloths, a sponge, a can of deodorant, soap, sanitiser, spare underwear, a diaper, spare trousers, a tee shirt and a refuse sack for soiled clothes. I learnt the hard way. No taxi will allow you to have a soiled refuse sack in his cab, nor you, if you stink. See below.

The Don'ts

Before you venture out. The night before or on the morning of your social interaction and you venture out, don't consume lots of eggs, runny foods, fizzy drinks, milk or laxatives.

The Hard Lesson

In this, I was the victim of my own circumstances. I had decided to have an eye test at my local opticians in Galway city, Ireland. I obeyed all my Doos and Donts, as above. My driver Mike dropped me off and wheeled me to the outlet. He asked if he could collect his wife while waiting for me? I said away you go and I will meet you in the car park of the shopping centre. He departed and I had a very satisfactory eye test. After the eye test, they offered to wheel me to the car park which I declined; my independent streak coming to the fore. I made it to the car park, a distance of about 500 yards, pulling my chair with my right foot and pushing with my right hand. Once in the car park, I sensed danger deep inside me; I needed a toilet break and that meant going back into the shopping mall. To get there I had to make my way up a very steep ramp, which I couldn't manage. After several attempts of going around in circles, called wheelies or Doughnuts I was told, lo and behold a lady in a wheelchair appeared by my side and asked if she could help me? I politely said no thank you, feeling very taken aback and surprised.

Off she went and another lady appeared who had noticed my dilemma and asked if she could help in any way? This girl was straight off the modelling ramp and drop-dead gorgeous, so I decided to ask her name and where she worked and got both. She was Jessica O' Malley from the west of Ireland and was my first introduction to www.croi.ie, which is now my Stroke Support group. Our relationship did not last long; I discovered months later that she ran off to Edinburgh with some canny potato farmer. Now that burst my bubble and my aspirations!

By this time, my bowel was about to explode and I said a silent prayer to myself. Squeezing my ass-hole and praying for a **NO FART!** or **NO SQUIRT!** because you can never trust them. Nature plays by its own rules. I pleaded with Jessica to get me to a loo, so we raced up and down the mall, looking for cleaning staff because all the loos had punch code locks on them. When we finally reached a loo,

I couldn't hold back my rear-end tsunami! Can you remember all the times when you had to queue in a line to use the loo? Crossing your legs, squeezing your AHT and praying? Then it's your turn and the rush through the door and you are in the loo, PHEW! I had got half-undressed before the dam burst and it went everywhere, all over me, the wheelchair, the floor.

So, now it was clean-up time. I could not use the washbasins in the WC because they were in a public area and I did not want to become a spectacle or an object of humour or derision. But more so, I wanted to respect the space for others. Fortunately, my ingenuity came to the fore.

Still in the cubicle, I looked at the cistern and said to myself I can't use the toilet bowl. Then I had a light bulb moment, problem solved. I removed the lid from the cistern; it contained as much water as I needed, with plenty of flushing and refilling the cistern, to clean myself, the wheelchair and the floor area. All my soiled clothes went into the black refuse sack which I left in the cubicle, told the cleaning attendant later and he disposed of them. I got dressed, sprayed and appeared outside where the lady was still waiting and we went our separate ways.

Next time you view someone in a wheelchair, don't feel sorry just think what if? Could it be me? Because all of the above is happening to someone, somewhere. My wheelchair saved me from having to have a STOMA, a bowel bag, as it would have been completely impractical for me. Brownie points for wheelchairs! YIPPEE!

6

Care Homes

Nursing homes, care homes, these are regulated skilled nursing facilities, providing residential care for:

1.   the elderly.

2.   the infirm.

3.   the disabled

4.   those with dementia.

5.   those who require respite or convalescence.

The Care Home has a mix of patients with different ailments:

1.   Alzheimer's

2.   Respite care needs

3.   Stroke

4.   Parkinson's

5.   Motor neuron

6.   Multiple sclerosis

7.   Disabled

8.   Cancer

9.   The infirm

10.   Mental Health issues

11.   Essential Tremors.

Given such a mix in the confined space of a care facility, all of us patients integrate really well with each other with little or no friction between us. The overall atmosphere is very serene with lots of mutual respect and harmony in evidence. No other patient will ever be informed as to why you are residing there. These facilities are teeming with LIFE.

The big day arrived for my transition to a Care Home. My two sons had done extensive research on locating and dealing with all the paperwork required and assured me that the chosen home would be perfect for me. Everything at this time is about team work and so it was up to me to play my part, to let go and trust their judgement.

I felt very apprehensive, as it was like leaving family members behind, mainly because of all the new friendships I had forged there. Tears were shed and the arrival at the care home was well-rehearsed; my incarceration was complete almost before I realised it.

To sweeten everything, while in my room with my sons, both shuffling around nervously, the time for their departure approaching because they had a long journey ahead of them, looking at watches and each other, a silent language going on, when on cue, the chef arrived with my supper, a sumptuous Indian curry, pre-arranged, from the local Indian restaurant. That brought a big smile, as I tucked in, almost unaware that my sons had departed. That was it, all settled in and content.

To add to my enjoyment, I had a bottle of red wine, Malbec, in my holdall. This was the way to settle in. While I was enjoying my tipple, Janet my house nurse arrived and looked at my glass.

"Right Dave," she said. "Where is the bottle?"

I gave it to her and she said:

"I will be back in one hour and you can have another glass, then two more for tomorrow evening."

This was an easy and great start! And not unique to me. You can do it too. It felt like a home from home. What is all the fuss about, regarding the transition to a care home? I asked myself that night after I had been tucked up in my new bed. I had the same process arranged for my current care home, where all the chefs are Indian and very innovative.

All About Care Homes

Nursing homes, care homes, are regulated skilled nursing facilities for the residential care of PETALS. They will provide all your prescribed medication to you on a daily basis.

What Is Meant by Convalescence?

When you convalesce, you heal or grow strong after illness or injury, often by staying off your feet.

What Is Meant by Respite Care?

Respite care may involve providing alternative family or institutional care for a person with a disability, in order to enable the carer to take a short break, a holiday or a rest. It can cover very short-term respite, for example, a carer for an evening, or a much longer arrangement for a holiday. In my experience, quite a number of respite long-term patients, while content in their care environment were very happy for it to be their final resting place and for their demise, rather than go home and not have the **Safety Net** of a care home.

Acceptance and Reassurance

Acceptance in human psychology is a person's and their loved ones' assent to the reality of a situation, recognising a process or condition often a negative or an uncomfortable one. Derived from the Latin: acquiēscere, to find rest in.

Acceptance doesn't mean you're accepting that it's going to be that way forever. There is no shame in surrender, only strength, fortitude and pride in having decided what is best for your body and your mental health, your peace of mind and that of your loved ones.

The grieving process, whether concerning the loss of a loved one or an issue such as leaving home, is about accepting what is, and letting go of what cannot be. Before I surrendered to acceptance, I was exhausted with self-pity at my misfortune and tired of fighting the anger of the perceived injustice of my tragedy, not to mention feeling ashamed for bringing this tragedy upon my family. However, three years later my world and its outlook are very different; care homes have played a huge role in my recovery process, both mentally and physically. So, don't be apprehensive. I should like to dismiss the misconceptions about care homes being institutions or end of life facilities. That's just idle gossip and I can assure you, is not true. And they are not new forever homes, just our new normal ones, our **Safety Net**.

Some people believe that acceptance is a sign of apathy, passivity, giving up; this is not true, it's only doing what is practical for all. However, this doesn't have to be the case. Practising acceptance does not necessarily mean you won't be able to make a change, as you still have choices You can accept your body and still change it; accept your emotions and acknowledge their impermanence and accept your behaviour one day because you might change it tomorrow. Acceptance doesn't mean you're accepting it's going to be that way forever. It's not permanent.

When you have chosen your care home, you should feel a deep sense of relief and gratitude within yourself as you prepare to start your new journey, as this is not your new forever home, it is your new normal one. So, when you sit at your bedside each morning, just think of yourself as a doughnut! Some people, when looking at a doughnut only focus on the hole, so focus on you, not the doughnut. In other words, take pride in your daily appearance and always try to look the best you can be. Try to be better than you were the day before. Be upbeat, be pleasant to everyone. As a resident, challenge yourself to know the names of the members of staff; they will feel very proud that you have made the effort to do so and you will be well-rewarded with TLC! If you have a bad attitude, get rid of it.

Remember, it is up to us to be safe; don't do what we should not do and put ourselves in danger. If in trouble, ring the bell.

Choosing a facility: which, where and why? Your options to choose from are Public, Private or Corporate.

1. Make an appointment to view and get a tour of the facility. Morning time is better as there is more going on within and more to see. Bring a nurse or similar professional with you. They will notice things that you may not.

2. Bring your loved one with you. Keep your opinions to yourself, as you are shown around. No "oohs" and "ahs" and don't try the hard sell on your loved one. Ask if they have any queries; discuss the visit later in a coffee shop or similar, in a cosy, relaxed atmosphere. When visiting and entering the busy residents' lounge area, it may appear that they are all staring at you. They are only noticing that you are new and different. Just ignore it. We are not being judgemental and when you move to another room, we will forget that we even noticed you. Don't be self-conscious.

3. Get a list of what you need to bring with you and get a list of the doos and donts within the home. Ask if you can bring some home furnishings and favourite things for your room?

4. Research reviews on Facebook and other social media platforms.

5. Ask to see their lunch and tea-time menus. You will notice a lot of egg-based dishes. This is to cater for those on soft diets. They won't do a la carte menus but will cater for you as best they can. Wherever you choose to go, give them a list of your preferred foods and what you don't like, such as gravy being poured all over your lunch when served up. Speak up at your residents' meetings as the chefs will be in attendance. The staff will bring the menus to your room if that is where you choose to dine. Bring your favourite sauces, toppings with you and keep them in your room fridge.

6. Are there local take-away food outlets close by? If so, visit them, get copies of their menus and keep these in your room for phone-in orders. Visit the local newsagent and arrange to have your favourite magazines etc delivered.

Where, Which and Why?

What is the difference between a nursing home and a long-term care facility?

Once they are deemed strong enough and stable, most patients may leave a skilled nursing facility to go home or into non-assisted/independent living, subject to medical approval. Long-term care facilities are often, small 2-bedroom cottages, part of a skilled facility. These are for patients who do not require hands-on care and supervision 24 hours a day and who can do with the services of nurses, aides and healthcare assistants, as required. If you are considering either type of facility, please do the following: read your contract very carefully and have it vetted by your solicitor and your family.

Public, Private or Corporate?

With hindsight, having been in all three to date, I went for Corporate the second time in that they have the muscle, being well-financed and will not be any more costly as most are on the same price level here in Ireland, overseas and all are overseen by government agencies and health departments. Private facilities went through a torrid time with mortalities, as did some public ones, with the current covid pandemic and deserve the opportunity to bounce back, which they will do as most are local.

Corporate homes appeared to have side-stepped large-scale Covid mortalities. I have no doubt that the private units will follow the corporate format, eventually, by bringing in private investors, just as BNBs did with hotel competition. This is big business, a real cash cow, overseen and regulated, with a portion of the patients' overheads paid directly and monthly by the government health department, which could be $2000 per patient by 100 patients in a home, which equals a lot of cash each month.

The atmosphere within the home is much more relaxed, as there are no visual signs of financial shortcomings and you are not looking at ashen-faced owners, dogged with their own woes, who themselves should be incarcerated, rather than imposing their dull and dour moods upon all of the staff, which in turn affects us, the real residents. Ultimately, a higher turnover of staff ensues which definitely affects some residents, because they can become attached as relationships develop and the disappointment can hurt deeply.

Corporate care homes have deep pockets and larger budgets and can afford to carry an extensive bank of skilled staff. Given the times we are in with the pandemic, they can afford top-quality nursing managers and nurses and can best react to the current situation of the Covid pandemic. They can provide the best patient equipment as deemed necessary and have less turnover of staff. I can assure you, that you are legally permitted to change to a different care home at your leisure, following all the necessary procedures.

Now, regarding the sensitive aspect of you or your loved one, making this huge decision, which can be very divisive, especially for family members, often causing heated arguments, the first hurdle is the acceptance of the inevitable for all concerned.

Your Acceptance Prayer:

"God grant me the serenity,
to accept,
the things I cannot change,
Give me the courage to change
the things I can,
and the wisdom,
to know the difference.

- Reinhold Niebuhr

Where?

1. Research its location. Is it within one hour of a major hospital with an A&E department? This is because, in the event of a stroke or a traumatic occurrence, you or your loved one will be within "The Golden Hour," to the nearest A&E necessary to prevent death, avoid additional brain damage and paralysis.

2. Is the facility close to a motorway for ease of access for family and friends?

3. Is it close to a town or village with transport facilities, such as taxi services, buses, trains and a shopping area, with church services?

4   It is important that the facility can easily access consultants, radiography services for X-rays, C.T scans and imagery, Ophthalmic, Dental and Medical services.

5.   Are there local take-away food outlets? Newsagents?

All of the above points should be noted by the older generation if considering moving home in their later years.

As I set out above, the most important factor is location, location, location. My first care home was very posh; it appeared to have all the bells and whistles and as we all know, if it's too good to be true, it's not. Consider this poem: "All that glistens is not gold." Remember the old adage: "look Before you leap." If you're not sure, request all of your family view the care home, make further appointments, save and update your list of questions and the assurances you would like, if you were to choose. Sign nothing until you and all family members are as sure as possible.

I found out the hard way when it was too late but I did get out and moved to a superior care home, not flashy, but you really can't judge in advance, because the success or failure of any care home is down to how they function within. There is no substitute for experience and they know it too because what you cannot see, cannot be!

In Ireland, all are overseen by government agencies and health departments. There are two contracts to be signed off: one for you, one for the landlord, both to be witnessed.

Beware

Some private care homes may try to obtain up-front payments in advance of their due date if their cash flow is under pressure or occupancy is low (for whatever reason). Don't be bullied; be sure to ensure that these provisions are discussed at the outset. Discuss any payment terms with your family and make sure to get the contract with the facility reviewed in advance. Like any other service, the detail is in the fine print!

Also, it is vital to record and report any disturbance, such as excess noise, outside or inside, to your facility and your family etc. Beware of any construction development plans not mentioned in the contract terms and which proceed and have an impact on you. Take whatever legal action is open to you; get legal advice and take photos of the exterior of the facility, just in case there is any development work commencing which you haven't been notified of in advance as this could affect the quality of your life in the future. Act Now and make sure to ask if there are any plans for substantial renovations or developments which may finish the quality of life you have. Nobody wants to listen to 8 hours of drilling per day!

I and many others like me have been subject to such uncomfortable and frustrating issues, in particular where the facility owner built above and below us and all around us, without any due concern for residents, many of whom may be very **ILL** and **DISTRESSED**.

It is important to recognise that these facilities are ultimately businesses with large overheads and when they are struggling, the first sign is that the food goes downhill, with poor food options, lesser quality and reduced portions. So, if they will not listen, seek appropriate advice (legal or otherwise), start a petition in-house and if you need to, don't be afraid to get it out there on social media. If you cannot do it, get a friend to do it for you. In my own experience, in one instance, it wasn't possible to get salads in the summertime, for instance. Then it was the in-house free services, such as entertainment, outings, hair dressing and the list goes on.

It's important to note that many operators are fantastically professional and really understand the needs of their residents and are interested in giving them the best quality of life possible. However, as in most things in life…there are those who have different motivations

7
Beyond the Front Door

Ground Floor

Most care homes are single storey buildings. This is where you will find: a salon for hairdressing; nail-bar; podiatry; consultancy; physio room and occupational therapy; recreation gardens; an oratory and a nursing station. The activity room has games, movies, arts and crafts, singing and choir practice.

Most care homes have zero tolerance concerning drinking alcohol in public areas. However, there is a holding area for your favourite tipple, which they will retain for you. Just ask your duty nurse to give you a 'wee dram' in your room before bedtime, cheers! As per the verses below, everything is not always what it appears to be. If it is too good to be true, then it's probably not. Be Alert! They are selling a service!

> *all that glistens is not gold—*
> *often have you heard that told.*
> *many a man his life hath sold*
> *but my outside to behold.*
> *gilded tombs do worms enfold.*
> *had you been as wise as bold,*

young in limbs, in judgment old,
your answer had not been inscrolled
fare you well. your suit is cold—

The first hurdle is joint acceptance of the inevitable by all parties.

Downstairs

1. Just inside is a reception/visiting area, with a tea and coffee station.

2. A large lounge with a library for residents

3. A TV room

4. Kitchen plus dining room

5. Activity room

6. Gardens

7. Exercise room

8. A salon for hairdressing, nail-bar, podiatry, consultancy, physio room and occupational therapy. recreation gardens. an oratory and a nursing station.

Daily Life Within

Most mornings are spent on the ground floor where all your activities take place, such as dining, the gymnasium room for exercise classes, art classes, the oratory and the library. The salon is used for any pre-booked appointments for hairdressing, podiatry, nail bar, reflexology, massage. You can also spend time in your garden, or in the potting shed doing gardening tasks, or for the more active, play Boccia, or for the smokers this area is your haven. No smoking is allowed anywhere in-house.

After supper, which may be either in the dining room or outdoors, such as a Barbecue in the garden in the summer time, you retire to your room or the communal room for a sing-along, watch golden oldies' movies or attend choir practice for Xmas time. You can have your favourite tipple served to you in your room, with your buddies.

Your facility may provide evening entertainment by local drama and music groups. Religious services may be provided by the local churches in the Communal room. Notifications of all events will be on the notice boards, throughout.

It is important that you attend your residents' meetings and don't feel intimidated about speaking up if you have issues. Your nursing manager and the chefs will attend. Ask to have a Suggestion Box provided for the shy residents and of course, a residents' chairperson for the meetings. Only they can open the suggestion box.

No matter where you are in the world, your care homes are overseen and regulated by government agencies. I am in Ireland.

The Downstairs Kitchen

This is the heartbeat of any care home. This is the gossip centre and your high street, so look smart. It never closes and is never empty. The kettle is always on and surprise goodies may appear. Interact with all of the care staff here. You need never, ever be lonely. Eat and drink as much as you can and no one is counting.

I once got in trouble there as I used to steal all the sliced bread for my bird friends every night. One morning, no one could have toast for breakfast as there was no bread to be had. A terrible hullaballoo followed with the big question: who was guilty? Anyway, they caught me on the cameras, as they are everywhere. I had a balcony outside my room and was visited by seagulls and crows on a daily basis; they loved the sliced bread. There are no big smart screen TVs in the kitchen dining area, only good conversation.

Crying Wolf

We have all heard the story of Crying Wolf and its consequences. In your room, you have a call bell for your security and safety. Use it with respect, consideration and caution. I always ask myself before I press the bell: Have I got a problem or a preference, or just being lazy? If you are male, have a urine bottle at your bedside for nighttime relief and empty it yourself if you can do it safely. If you are a Piddling Pete, ask for a second bottle and make sure you rinse them out with water, otherwise, you may end up with an Itchy Willie, as there is a lot of salt in urine! Bring your own urine bottle to the care home and put your room number on it for in-house sterilisation.

Upstairs

24 Bedrooms, nurses' stations, kitchenette, sluice room, laundry room, residents' communal room, corridor.

Challenges within are incontinence; fitness and obesity; exercise your sphincter muscle, the ass-hole, daily, by squeezing it, while you are sitting for long periods of time. This will prevent leakages and squirts and being called the Smelly One. It will also make your pelvic floor stronger, which will enhance your copulation performances, your thrust. This applies to both male and female.

Cocooning, as we all did during Covid 19; learning to like your own company and how best to entertain yourself.

Fight incontinence. Using diapers for many is an easy but lazy option. Be conscious of the fact that they do leak and smell, which can be uncomfortable for fellow residents, family and friends when in your company. There are a number of brands of specialised underwear. Speak to your doctor or in-house nurses. If you can beat the challenge of incontinence, then you can fly, go on foreign holidays, without being concerned about those around you. At times, it may feel somewhat degrading when the care staff have to rig you up on a hoist to change your diaper. There is a sense of helplessness about it, shame and guilt. Most infirm patients can't change it themselves. The staff do have to lift and manoeuvre you in the bed, so I overcame incontinence and smiled. I told everyone I could beat it. Wearing a diaper inside your pants can make your backside look like the rear of a wide bus; not attractive from any angle!

Obesity

Being overweight is your only enemy here, as you can become unbalanced and may fall over, very easily resulting in serious injuries such as a head injury, fractured hips, or legs, or arms. It's all up to ourselves, as we are what we eat. I eat two heads of lettuce each day and it really burns off the calories. You will be weighed on the first day of every month and you cannot avoid it or hide. There are lots of places to exercise, such as your garden and along all the corridors within the care homes, all of which have safety rails up to 50 meters long. If you get tired and not sure you can make it back to your room, there are always assistants or cleaning staff along the corridor who will come to your aid. Don't ask a fellow resident for physical assistance, just stay where you are and wait. If you are not able, you will not be allowed to do it on your own, so ask for permission first; no solos or heroes here; and no slipping off the toilet. Regarding exercise, do small sections each day and build.

Your Room

This is the most important room in the facility, as it is your new home for a while, not your new forever home. However, pretend that it is because most places will allow you to decorate it, as you please, allowing you to bring in some favourite furnishings from home, such as an armchair, dressing table, pictures, posters etc, which will be hung for you. You can have your own table and standard lamps.

All rooms are off long corridors and are rectangular in shape, with lots of light coming in through picture windows and garden areas outside of your window. Rooms are painted in pastel colours which are easy on the eye. Have your own duvets, throws, cushions, pillows or blankets; bring them. Anything that will add to your comfort and the quality of living within. You will also have a locker, with a drawer that will have a key; wear it around your neck for safekeeping. Keep wallets, valuables, chargers in that drawer but not cash; you can leave that at reception. Lend nothing to anybody, as you will surely never see it again.

You can have Sky TV and your own internet provider installed once you arrange it and let management know. Anything electrical, let the in-house maintenance team know so that they can check it for safety. You can have your own big smart screen TV fitted. Be noise conscious daytime or evening, for your fellow residents.

You will have a nice practical bathroom en-suite. Your room will be cleaned each day by the cleaners who are very friendly and chatty. If you have a staff favourite, they may not always be available to you as they are part of a team. Make them all your favourites and you will never be disappointed. Your room will never be locked, while you are inside.

Your laundry will be collected daily and duly returned, as each item has your room number tagged on it. So, no need to be concerned at any time. When they return it, they will check each item with you to ensure it's yours.

Another essential to add to your overall comfort: arrange to have a mini-fridge in your room, to store your sodas, bottled water and soft fruits. This adds another layer to your in-house independence. You can have cases of bottled water and more delivered by local stores and supermarkets. In my case, the care home chef orders all my goodies directly from Musgraves' store for me, so it can work for everyone. Just plan well in advance. Bring your favourite wine glass from home. You may have up to 40 visitors a day to your room between nurses, their aides, assistants, cleaning staff etc. so, make it nice and inviting for them. This is part of your passage back to independent living. So, keep your room looking well-organised as people will notice this ability of yours and you'll rake up the brownie points!

Dining in Your Room

All homes cater for this and it is very satisfying; you can also have a buddy join you for dining. I dine alone all of the time and you do not miss out on anything, except idle chat. And you can have your glass of vino which is not allowed to be consumed in public areas.

Your room is your bolt-hole. You have your own bathroom en-suite. Give your loved ones a list of the takeaway restaurants of your choice in the vicinity. I visit them all and get copies of their menus. You can consume these in the privacy of your own room and maybe share them with someone. Tell the receptionists that you are expecting a delivery and let them pay for it out of your cash kitty.

Care Home Suitcases

His Bag: 3 pairs of large boxers, to accommodate a diaper; slippers; shorts; tracksuit bottoms; tee-shirts; washbag; Rescue Bag, for outdoor treats with family etc; formal wear, suit etc; shoes. It will also contain a long-necked urine bottle; put your room number on it; phone chargers, etc; a nice photo for your room door; a suit for formal wear and smart casuals.

Her Bag: 3 large knickers to accommodate a diaper; slippers; shorts, etc; a wash and a Rescue Bag; formal wear etc; phone chargers etc; a nice photo for your room door. Add more of your own.

For All: With cocooning and spending a lot of time sitting for most of our days, we are susceptible to having rashes in our groin and arm-pit areas, caused by movement of clothing and shuffling in our seating. So, it is good to have your own self-help cures, such as Sudo-crème and Caldesine powder, on the premise that prevention is better than cure and self-help is definitely best. Rather than calling for a nurse all the time, think should I ring the bell? Have I a problem or a preference, or will I be crying wolf?

While sitting, everyone can exercise their sphincter muscle (your ass-hole). Just keep squeezing it as often as you can, as it is also a great exercise for your pelvic floor muscles, even for those on the outside who may do a lot of driving. It also helps to prevent leakages and being smelly and saves you a lot of money on incontinence products!

The Reception Area

This is staffed by office professionals, who will gladly assist you with all your IT issues, photocopying and so on. They can also mind some cash for you, known as your kitty and account for it.

Mental Health Issues

Let us have a conversation, about nothing in particular! Just a chat! about nothing! and a smile and a laugh in between!

Those whom I have met within the nursing home are very happy and contented because they always have companionship and never feel isolated. They integrate seamlessly and are kept busy doing artwork and other related activities. Don't forget, your body also needs iron to make some hormones. As a result, iron deficiency anaemia may leave you tired and short of breath and with aching muscles, post-exercise.

Having chosen your care home, you have assented to the reality of your current situation, without protest or resistance, as you truly say yes to the new quality of life that may embrace you and you surrender your previous one of torment. This is your new norm. Listen to the Niall Breslin podcast: "Where is my mind?"

So, what is next for you? Now that you are a resident and are familiar with routines such as mealtimes, attempt to create a daily routine for yourself. Always try to cooperate with the staff. Have breakfast in your room, then go to the kitchen for extras. Your room is your castle; put up your pictures and more. My first prayer every day is to be better than I was yesterday and to have a good attitude today. Never have a bad attitude.

It is essential to have goals; mine is to return home and experience independent living. Exercise within the home or gardens is essential and social, to avoid obesity and its complications and to talk. While in the home, you are your own master and you can't be compelled to do things that you do not wish to do. You will find this huge gift of partial independent living, allows you the freedom to live life fully, because up to now, you were not really living, just existing and you can now do most things that you would like to do, such as going to a movie, theatre, restaurants and so on, together with family, friends, or with a healthcare assistant for safety,

Keep your room tidy; show off your organising skills. The cleaners will be in with you every day. Ensure you have windows open and that your room always smells fresh and inviting. Being on our own, we can sometimes forget this aspect and respect for others; for instance, with your room smelling like a pigsty from farting like a trooper! Always be considerate and conscious of others, visiting your room on a daily basis. You do not want your room referred to as the Stinky One by the staff and visitors. No candles are allowed in rooms, however, aroma diffusers are welcomed.

8

Our Caregivers

Lest we forget: nursing and care homes and hospitals, we use these words in our daily lives, flippantly, without too much regard for the nurses and healthcare assistants, cleaners, porters, kitchen staff, without whom, none would function. In the Covid pandemic worldwide they were being showered with plaudits and bouquets for their sterling work as front-liners in the eye of the storm. They are still paid miserly salaries and yet our expectations of them are often presumed, expected and thankless, STILL. They are Still paid miserly salaries and yet our expectations of them are Still presumed.

While in hospital and in the care home, I watched these people come into work every morning and I began to ask myself, would I do what they do on a daily basis? Would you haul yourself out of your hot Horny romantic bed, leave your partner and children, to come into work and attend to us? Shower us, clean our butts? More often than not, they go beyond the call of duty for us care home residents, to enhance our well-being with a smile. They see life in us, something most do not see and we can make them smile too, which they love. We all know that life is a gift to be treasured and our caregivers nurture it around the clock, everywhere in the world and we have reason to smile for every extra gifted moment.

A true **short story**: in Lourdes, a healthcare assistant on being asked by an eminent stranger, seeing all the bodies on the stretchers being moved to and from the baths: "Why do you do this work every day, carrying all these people to and fro?" She replied: "We see what you can't see. We see and feel the life in them!" All petals.

**A thank you to all carers,
everywhere in our universe.**

Claire wrote this whilst walking on the beach, yesterday: "Before my own day's work as a nurse, as the sun was rising, I was thinking and praying for my Dad who has dementia and for all of you who live and work in his world every day, all of you who bring me hope for a better tomorrow in my world, because of your hearts that care, your hands that touch and your eyes that twinkle, with laughter and mischief; your soft voices that reassure my Dad, when he feels slightly more lost and further away. Each and every one of you is to Dad what I can't be, because of distance and life and I want to say a heartfelt thank you for giving me the reassurance, that Dad's world is better than good. He is safe, happy, his days are filled with laughter and joy. I know only too well, that in doing what you do, especially at this time with the pandemic, of so much unknown and your own daily overriding of fears and having the courage to make sacrifices and in doing what you do, you give me the gift of hope and for all of this, I say thank you."

- Claire Auchmuty, Denzel's daughter

Hope is…?

A PERSON.

Hope has breath

Hope has Life and is Life

Hope brings change

Hope breathes Life

Hope strengthens

Hope sustains

Hope lifts and carries

Hope supports and is yet strong

Hope bends and is unbreakable

Hope will not let us down or fail us

Hope will never die or disappear

Hope rises up and endures

Hope believes, sees and hears

Hope reaches out and draws in and lives forever

Hope now sticks by my side

Hope is constant and yet ever-changing

H = hang

O = on

PE = persist

Hope = Hang On, Persist!

9
Doos and Don'ts for Visiting Your Loved One

Doos

Let him or her and the people at reception know in advance, the time and day of your proposed visit and if there are plans to go out for lunch or tea. This is to ensure that the person is suitably attired and the nurses will have him or her all powdered and puffed and ready for you. Check their cash balance while waiting at reception. Top it up and tell your loved one. If you have a parcel or present leave it with staff at reception, who will arrange to have it delivered to the relevant room. Most have a reception area for coffee, teas and scones. Keep your conversation low in this area, as walls have ears and it is best to have discussions elsewhere.

Someone at reception will notify your loved one that you have arrived and he or she will be duly wheeled to the reception area. If you are going to their room, respect their privacy by knocking on the door first. If they are being attended to by staff in their room, please excuse yourself and wait in the adjacent corridor. Check their funds situation while at reception and try to speak with the senior nurse on duty; request this in advance of your visit, as they are very busy, with regard to any issues your loved one may have.

Try to be smiley and jovial and relay any local gossip pertaining to their friends or people they know. Don't mollycoddle too much, softly touch and hold their hands. You and other friends should send cards and presents from Amazon. You should see their eyes light up like headlamps on receiving such a surprise! Don't think about it, just do it. Keep the conversation light-hearted and positive.

Bring them their favourite treats, such as punnets of blueberries, strawberries, raspberries, blackberries, as there tends to be little or no fruit or salads available. Bring their favourite tipple which will be dispensed by their nurse, each evening after supper. Spend time with them in the garden.

Sky TV

Patients will be allowed to have this installed in their room with the relevant channels they would like. The younger staff members will help them navigate the channels and their preferred programmes. You can also bring DVDs, which can be viewed on the smart TV in their room.

Remind them, that all their medication will be dispensed to them twice daily. They can request paracetamol if so required. They are not allowed to purchase any medication elsewhere, such as online nor keep any in their room.

Don'ts While Visiting Your Loved One

Don't argue with them. No matter what ails them, you can't agree with them but let them see you are listening and that you will address their concerns. Do that with their nurse later on the phone. Don't arrive with unruly pets, or children, as they can get very agitated if overwhelmed. Make sure your pet's health is ok and that their shots are validated; have the certificate with you. If your loved one is sleeping when you arrive, leave them be. If woken, they may feel groggy and may be tetchy!

We patients – our Doos and Donts

1. Be pleasant, polite and welcoming to your visitor.

2. No whinging. No dramatics.

3. No moaning!

4. Be sensitive to your visitor and if you have any little requests for their next visit, tell them.

5. Stay safe within your room. Take no risks

6. Press the bell if you need assistance. Is it a problem or a preference?

7. No over-use of the words "I" or "me".

8. Don't visit at mealtimes. Always call in advance, which is only good manners, after all.

- Don't have large groups of family and/or friends visit at the same time. This may overwhelm other residents or make them anxious. How many visitors are too many? This will be different for every resident. Observe your loved one's mood and try to determine if there are too many people visiting. Don't have visits at or before mealtimes, as this may lead to anxiety.

If you are feeling tired, tell your visitors.

- Do not interrupt the resident's activity time. Find out from the staff when activities are scheduled. It may be acceptable to sit beside them unless your presence distracts them from the activity. You can get guidance from the staff.

10
Doos And Don'ts For Our Loved Ones

Doos for Interacting with Staff

- Learn the names of staff members involved in your loved one's care and be warm in your interactions with them. Thank them for any special services.

- If the facility has visiting hours, respect them. Otherwise, you may impede the staff from carrying out their caregiving duties.

- Keep the lines of communication open. Should there be a problem, communicate it promptly and directly to the administrator or the director of nursing. Never confront an aide directly.

- Attend the regularly scheduled care conferences to which you are invited. This is a good time to discuss your wishes or concerns about the care your loved one is receiving and get updates on how he or she is doing. This is a good time to discuss your wishes or concerns for your loved one is receiving and get updates on how he or she is "settling in" and adapting to life in the care home.

11

Don'ts for Interacting With Staff

- Don't order the staff around. If you have requests, talk to the director of nursing or the administrator, depending on the nature of the request.

- Don't give tips or bring gifts for the staff if the facility has guidelines forbidding them. Check with the staff about their policy. Some facilities allow holiday gifts. If no gifts are allowed, give handwritten thank you cards to those you want to recognize.

Tipping and presents: most homes discourage individual staff from receiving gifts. It's best to provide a hamper for all the staff.

- Don't be a chronic complainer. It's like crying wolf. Before you request attention, ask yourself if it's really a problem or a preference?

- Don't have unrealistic expectations. Understand that staff have many patients to care for and may not have time to do every tiny thing you'd like. Again, before complaining, make sure it's a problem, not just a preference.

• Don't visit at mealtime unless you have checked with the administrator regarding the facility's policies. Some nursing homes welcome visitors to dine with their loved ones, others do not.

Following these simple guidelines will help you avoid problems that could occur. It will also make your visits far more pleasant for everyone.

12

Miscellaneous and Random Notes

Here are some thoughts, quotes and tit-bits, that I picked up over the last four years, as I shuffled along the highways, by-ways, cul-de-sacs and blind alleyways of my mind. These amused me and gave me some mental stimulation, amid cocoon-ism, isolation and the dark, black tunnels on a daily basis. Uplifting positivity comes to my mind, ending in a floodlit space: a care home that functions as it should and does what it says on the tin!

Those of us who have survived our afflictions or traumas have good reason to smile with the world which is a symbol of friendship and peace. Nothing can be done without hope and confidence. Health is our greatest gift but it is very fragile and should be nurtured with contentment, loyalty and faithfulness, both of which best describe what friendship is. Success is the result of perfection, hard work, loyalty, determination, persistence and will power. Nothing can be done without love and affection in your world. Optimism is the faith, that leads to achievement. Always maximize your full potential and put meaning into everything you do.

Now and then, look at yourself and ask: who am I? The will to win is the desire to succeed and the urge for you to maximise your full potential. These are the keys that will allow you to unlock the pathways to your own personal excellence and your personality to blossom because that is you. Do the right things, progress will move on, you will gratify some and yourself and astonish the rest! Humour is mankind's greatest blessing, so we need to embrace it and join in.

Never be afraid to ask. Asking can be a compliment because you would never ask a villain! Unless you are one yourself. Do something every day that you want to do. This is the golden rule for acquiring the result of doing your duty without pain. I can teach anybody how to get what they want out of life but nobody can tell me what they want. Do you? Don't wait, the time will never be right. It is easier to find out than to suppose. Wisdom is the reward we get for a lifetime of listening when we would rather have spoken.

The two most important days in our lives are the day we were born and the day we found out why? Never allow someone else to be your priority while allowing yourself to be their option and if you tell the truth, you don't ever have to remember anything. Contentment comes from the value of joy when you have someone to share it with. The only animal that blushes is man. Get your facts first and then distort them at your leisure. Don't lean on your family too much; control your own affairs and be accountable. One has a duty to their expectations, such as acceptance, not venting, not doing as you should do. No bad attitude; don't be a pain in the ass.

Of all the **POSITIVES** of care home living, I have found that the **PEACE**, **PRIVACY**, **SILENCE** and **TRANQUILLITY** we get to enjoy daily are very uplifting. Time is something we have much more of every day and are never short of it, if only we could bank it. We just don't think about it, as we do not need to; we just have to live and enjoy life, peace, privacy, silence.

Time is something you can gain again if you go with the rules, being involved in all the activities and exercise, creating a daily regime for yourself. Keep busy, that is better than any medication, which is preventative. Your words and daily interaction with staff will be to your advantage as they are your window to the outside world, beyond your four walls. Right now, amidst any pandemic, your hospital or care home bed is the safest place on our planet to be.

Never trust your feelings because they keep changing! The lifeforce within you is what makes you the person you are. Your personality fills up the rest of what is only an **Empty Shell**. If you consider that you have a clear conscience, then that is a sure sign of a bad memory! The best way to cheer yourself up is to make someone else happy. Of all the things I have lost, I treasure my mind the most, hence with this book, you, the reader a stranger to me, have been the source of my inspiration and stimulation. Thank you, I do hope it has been helpful?

You can't depend on your eyes when your imagination is out of focus! Your eyes are the windscreen of your health to the world. Clinicians claim to know a lot but they really don't, as physios, in particular, are very anti-change and the introduction of technology, as they were not taught it in the classroom. Most will never complete their journey with you, as they neither have the time nor resources to see it through. Our journeys may be long but there are no records to break nor medals to win; just to be a re-united family again is the ultimate reward. So, we started, let us cross the finishing line together and meet our families and friends beyond the tape! Well done, to you all.

A Sure-Fire Tip

Make an effort to know the names of all your nurses, physios, healthcare assistants (aka angels), cleaners, kitchen staff; all feel very humbled when you have made the effort to know their names. It is practice and good therapy for your mind.

Recommended Reading

"Fish!: A Proven Way to Boost Morale
and Improve Results"
Novel by Stephen C. Lundin, a real morale booster!

"Come Back Early Today: A Memoir of Love, Alzheimer's and Joy"
by Marie Marley.

This book tells the powerful 30-year love story of a young American woman and a delightfully colourful, wickedly eccentric Romanian gentleman and scholar, interspersed with advice and inspiration for Alzheimer's caregivers everywhere

Marie Marley is the award-winning author of 'Come Back Early Today: A Memoir of Love, Alzheimer's and Joy' and the co-author of 'Finding Joy in Alzheimer's: New Hope for Caregivers.' Her website contains a wealth of information for Alzheimer's caregivers.

13

Useful Services

Flint Rehabilitation Devices, www.flintrehab.com

21 Useful Stroke Exercises to Improve Mobility and Function at Home

Enquiries to: dave.gero@gmail.com (Ireland)

Stroke, help in Ireland:

www.irishheart.ie

www.croi.ie I am a member of the stroke support group there.

www.headway.ie for Acquired brain injury.

The UK: www.bhf.org.uk

www.mystrokeguide@stroke.org,uk

14

In Conclusion

Today, 18.03.2020, I am still paralysed, happy and content in my care facility. Never be afraid of dying, if you have lived a full life.

Having been so fortunate as to survive my stroke, given that only10% of patients in my condition do, I promised myself to find a way of giving back. For instance, some proceeds from this will go to stroke charities. So, please spread the word, even with idle gossip!

When I started my journey in 2018, I felt like a nobody as I looked like a corpse in my bed, lying there with neither feelings nor substance, just hollow. Nobody is perfect and I didn't feel perfect in mine. Today in 2021, I am perfect, because I found somebody and it's me because every day I open my eyes and see the daylight, I know I have beaten my own record for the number of consecutive days for staying alive, 0 to72 and it feels great to be an achiever and somebody again. It just goes to prove hope is eternal and more often than not, it's in our own control. I wouldn't have got this far without care homes. Now 72 to100, please wish me luck!

Your body also needs iron to make some hormones. As a result, iron deficiency anaemia may leave you tired and short of breath and aching muscles, post-exercise.

All the money in the world could not pay for the peace, privacy, silence and tranquillity, that I get to enjoy every day, due to a stitch that I dropped in the Embroidery of my Life.

I should like to offer you all some tit-bits of useful information which may be beneficial in the course of your collective journey, as a team, which is all about give and take for both sides and ultimately acceptance and having let go.

My current and excellent nursing home is Mowlam Healthcare.com, whose staff do care and do listen. If a care home adds one extra moment to your lifespan, then it is worth going to one. Care homes are not end of life facilities or New Forever homes.

The following is a must-have for anyone going into hospital or a care home, or even travelling abroad. If you and your loved ones are serious internet users, then you must bring a Vodafone dongle with you. This is mobile broadband at its best. In most locations, the in-house internet can have glitches in relation to the signal to your room, or have none at all. This dongle has been my get out of jail card for 14 years, touring Ireland and abroad. It is not overly expensive, just don't use it for downloading. Keep its password in a safe place and just keep the credit on it topped up. You'll not regret it, as it can be used anywhere.

A few words of wisdom that help me get through each day. Plateau is not a failure, just a phase in our recovery! Slow progress is better than no progress.

Sitting on the edge of my bed each morning, my first thoughts for the day ahead are: have a good attitude; practice self-awareness, this will keep you safe; be better and look better today than you did yesterday. Take pride in your daily appearance, good self-awareness with safety will prevent any setbacks in your daily life. Check the area at your bedside, which can often look like an obstacle course, with wires, shoes, slippers, bed elevator, rubbish-bin, clothes and more.

The difference between a successful person and others is not the lack of knowledge or strength, but a lack of willpower; avoid the anxiety of expectation and your turn will come to fledge and fly. Don't be afraid of dying if you have lived. Hell is not about fire and brimstone, hell is all about your regrets in the life you have left behind. If you love someone, tell them now, rather than regret it later. Always try to be unselfish and thoughtful to those all around you each day.

Another essential to add to your overall comfort: arrange to have a mini-fridge in your room, to store your sodas, bottled water and soft fruits. This adds another layer to your in-house independence. You can have cases of bottled water and more delivered by local stores and supermarkets. In my case, the care home chef orders all my goodies directly from Musgraves for me, so it can work for everyone. Just plan well in advance. Advise those at reception about any deliveries that are due to arrive for you, as everything coming in has to be sanitized, for in-house safety.

My reflections on 2020. This project, the book, commenced on the morning of the 19th January 2018. As I emerged from my induced coma and the prospect of 72 hours to live, realizing the magnitude of my condition, that I was paralysed but thankfully with no cognitive issues. My sons needed all of my codes and passwords, well I spilt them out like a parrot.

I promised myself to find a way to give back to others less fortunate. I could see all the other acute patients in my ward and in a worse condition than me. Walking isn't everything; I would have met Covid 19 by now and wouldn't be typing this today due to my underlying conditions, but probably in a university morgue awaiting the new student medical year for dissection purposes and the scientific research into priapism!

For me, 2020 with Covid meant I had to be isolated at all times and so I became a one-handed keyboard jockey. So, let us forget about 2020 or at least parts of it although some people, of course, will never be able to do this. From the onset of the virus in springtime to now, with countless lockdowns, gate and door temperature checks, warning signs everywhere, extensive negative news bulletins worldwide, hearty laughs and chuckles behind visors and facemasks, we have learned to smile with our eyes and gained new perspectives on what is important in our daily lives.

We care home residents and our carers have endured difficult times with much anxiety regarding the welfare of our loved ones and our health. So, let us never lose this awareness and always greet the dawn of every day and smile at the sunset each evening. We care home residents and our welfare grabbed all the headlines around the world. We are not minorities any more. There is a whole new awareness and mindfulness of our generation! Yippee!

From the outset of this book, I have reminded you of the importance of having goals as you set off on your journey. Never be hesitant to change your goals. Initially, mine was to get from 69 to 71 and now I'm 72. My new goal is to go home in 2021, make the 100 and be involved in a number of ventures.

Since my stroke, I have a blood test every month, to verify the iron levels in my blood and to avoid future issues as before. You do the same. Ten minutes out of your day and maybe avoid two tragedies: one for you and one for your loved ones. Don't forget the PSA TEST, or be known as 'one hung low' with the limp!

My sons urged me to stay alive for their weddings and for any grandchildren and not to be a face in a wooden photo frame on the walls of their homes and saying to their kids: That was your Grandad! As my parents are to them.

So, they want living memories which is a heck of a compliment. Hence my acceptance and letting go to be here with Mowlam Healthcare, which has added to the quality and longevity of my life. We owe it to our next generation to let go and be part of their bigger family, rather than just a distant memory.

FINALLY DEAR READER, just like YOU, I always looked forward to a happy ending in a book, leaving me with a **Smile**. So I am, not going to disappoint you. Here is my news:

1.   I have a wedding invitation to my eldest son's wedding in a months time (July 2021).

2.   To bear witness to my 1st Grandchild!

3 .   The "**ALL CLEAR**" to return home.

4.   The pending arrival of a new "PET" (an English Springer Spaniel).

Well, I hope I brought You that **SMILE!** And thank you for your patience and persistance.

PHEW!!!! We got this far together!

I hope your journey is not as dramatic as mine, but that you will have as successful a conclusion as mine!

Spiritualism

Prior to my stroke, I had disconnected more or less from my Catholic faith. However, on reflection post my stroke, I realized I needed to get back in line and so I did and have become quite spiritual. Initially, I was back-tracking to all the saints I used to call upon as required: St Jude for hopeless cases. During the past few years, I have been collecting new saints like confetti. So, one morning, I said to myself, there are too many of them to pray to at one sitting, so I bundled them into one package like a TV box set and now refer to them as the Wisdomites. So, when you call on one of them, you are calling on all of them. They are brilliant and do work, just add your own list to my Wisdomites!

Prayer

Here is a special prayer for you; it is the favourite one of Pope John 23rd.

> *Every day I need you, Lord, but today especially,*
>
> *I need some extra strength to face whatever is to come.*
>
> *This day, more than any other day,*
>
> *I need to feel you near me to strengthen my*

Courage and to overcome any fear.

By myself, I cannot meet the challenge of the hour.

We are frail human creatures and we need a Higher Power to sustain us in all that life may bring.

And so, dear Lord, hold my trembling hand.

Be with me, Lord, this day and stretch out your powerful arm to help me.

May your love be upon me as I place all my hope in you. Amen.

A Very Special Care Home Memory

I would never have completed this book without the safety net of a care home because had I been allowed home, Mister Covid Virus would have buried me by now. I had met Father Jim - we were care home pals - in the kitchen one morning.

"Jim," I said. "I need you to hear my confession."

"Ok," he replied. "Let's do it in the lift! God will get it quicker if we go to the next floor."

I was delighted and so, into the lift, I pressed 2 and spilled the beans to Jim. I had to recite: "Jesus is good," for my penance throughout the day.

When we got out of the lift, Jim turned to me saying that it had been very uplifting, the confession express! We chuckled. He went off and he died two days later! RIP Jim.

What's Next for Me?

- A children's book on Christmas for 2021/2022.

- Back to arranging tours of Ireland: david.cong.1120@gmail.com

- Return home to www.connemara.ie and www.thewildatlanticway.com

- I will be arranging respite tours to a European venue for families and their loved ones at a professional rehab centre from 2022. Details from <u>dave.gero@gmail.com</u>

- Use Flintrehab.com and me, their agent @ dave.gero@gmail.com

- To raise money for a stroke-dedicated ambulance for the West of Ireland, which for those who may be affected, would be outside of the range of their "golden hour."

- All my proceeds will go to stroke foundations ref; DG - dave.gero@gmail.com

15

Let Us Reflect

On Care Homes

So, what do we all know now?

They are managed and run by skilled healthcare professionals.

They do listen and care.

Each one of all mankind will occupy a bed in these facilities at some time in their lives, as none of us can halt the clock of age or infirmity. It is our destiny! This will be your new normal and is mine now and for many like me!

As with hospitals, they function like well-oiled machines, that embrace the full cooperation of their residents. Don't be a wolf-crier, or you might have your tail docked.

The local hospitals and consultants work very much in tandem with the care homes.

They are not:

1. Institutions, or end of life facilities.

2. They are not your new forever homes.

3. Most don't have double beds but like most things, that can be arranged if they have larger rooms.

We as Residents

1. Have a duty of care to cooperate within the facility, with staff and fellow residents.

2. Be involved and be reasonable at your residents' meetings, as ultimately the outcomes and agreements are to the benefit of all. Be patient with the speed of progress; don't be the rowdy one! they do have red and yellow cards!

3. Don't lean on your families too much on a daily basis. When conversing with them, ban the use of the words I and Me right now. They are doing as much as they can do for you and like you and me, they are not qualified jugglers, so think before you talk! Think about the chat you might have and avoid all potholes, trouble issues. Your families are probably paying for your care, your consultant's fees, health insurance, your holidays, which you will have and your quality of life now is a whole lot better than it was. No more brown envelopes on a Monday or at the end of each month to concern yourself with. Excitement is permitted, for the bold, daring and brave!

4. If you are the randy type and you have a lover on the outside or inside, you both can meet on the outside at a local hotel, restaurant, theatre, bar, etc. It's great fun but don't come back to the home pixilated and singing! It's very important that you create a good relationship with a local taxi driver who you can cultivate as your 'wing man' and that he or she and you too can keep your moonlighting to yourself and your mouth airtight, as everywhere has sneaks and tell-tale tattlers. Here I am for one, telling you all of this. Shame on me!

Over to you. Go for it! with no regrets, only wry smiles.

Let Us Reflect on Our Medics
- Doctors, Surgens, Physios, Nurses And Healthcare Assistants

Very few of the above will complete your journey with you, nor will they try to push you beyond your limitations. We are not in a race or a competition but we do have a burning ambition to cross a line to where our loved ones are waiting for us.

My first care home, having previously been a hotel, was very flashy, which prompted me to recite the poem: All that glistens is not gold. Within a few months, the cracks appeared in their system and I am now somewhere new and very happy! I always cringed at the thought of going into a care home, No Never, Ever, Not me! Having often visited people in such places, I never felt comfortable with the thought of being in one myself. However, it can be a very serene and happy environment and I now find I have time, silence and privacy for me. There are no deadlines here, only appointments.

Set yourself goals before and while inside because you now have more time than you have ever known. To date, mine is to write 3 books and make it to a hundred years of age to collect my cheque from our president. I'm now seventy-two and with this lifestyle plus all the TLC, it's not false optimism, so wish me well.

The environment tends to be very serene and friendly with good interaction between staff and patients, with the opportunity to make new friends at mealtimes, activity sessions, the hairdressing salon, nail-bar, podiatry, a gym and lounge conversation areas. If heaven can be a little like this, I will gladly settle for this utopia, eternally!

Regardless of your personality, I guarantee you will find many a kindred spirit. These places are filled with life, characters and entertainers so, get involved and you will be very happy. There are no worries here, no enemies, no debt collectors, no criminals! It's like we have been gathered up in a big safety net, with all the world's problems on the outside.

My reflection now is that I am a living miracle, having survived my stroke, sleep apnea, electrocution, hypothermia and bowel cancer. So, why would I not be happy in my new skin and appreciate my new life, as opposed to no life at all as a cadaver?

I am not a trailblazer but I did invite my local police chief to one of our residents' meetings, to reassure people of their rights as senior citizens. We all loved it and felt reassured by it as did the care home staff and we experienced a new feeling of serenity within. After the success of that, we invited a pharmacist to explain the necessity of taking our medication and the reasons why. Finally, we had the one we all love to hide from, the dreaded physiotherapist. I can assure you that I have not seen any evidence that these care homes do, in any way, create an end-of-life environment, quite the opposite, in that they very much prolong life and they hum within the life of the living. We treasure our loved ones, our families and friends and they treasure us. All of us only have a loan of each other, so every extra moment together is very valuable, for all.

Outside services are permitted such as reflexology, massage and neuro physio practitioners visit you in the privacy of your own room. Also, you can have books and audio CDs delivered from the local library or from your local mobile library. They also have very good in-house laundry services, with all your clothes tagged on your arrival.

The "male suitcase" otherwise known as large boxer shorts, help accommodate a diaper and also prevent you from getting rashes in your groin area, due to long periods of sitting. The "female suitcase" has large knickers to accommodate a diaper. My list also included socks (2 pairs), t-shirts (6), formal wear for visits etc., slippers, shoes, shirts (2), lap-top, chargers and phone. We're advised never to loan anything out and ask a family member to record all our family and friends' phone numbers in a diary.

16

Reminders for All

On the Outside & The Inside

1.   Monthly blood tests for your iron, haemoglobin and oxygen levels in your Blood. Your body also needs iron to make some hormones. As a result, iron deficiency anaemia may leave you tired and short of breath and aching muscles, post-exercise.

2.   For him, his annual PSA test, or be 'one hung low' with a limp.

3.   Your sphincter muscle; squeeze it 1000 times a day, when sitting, driving, walking etc. you will avoid incontinence and leakages in years to come and save money on Tena and the likes. Avoid wearing crevice masks or thongs for unwanted leakages and squirts. Work on the sphincter, squeeze it and squirt no more!

4.   No bad attitude!

5.   Regular eye tests. What you cannot see, you cannot be.

6. Don't be anaemic, it can kill you. Have your blood tests. Break the mould; let go of your certainties.

F.A.S.T.

Signs for stroke; which is silent; are **F.A.S.T.** One every two seconds globally. Be alert and practise what if? Know your house code.

F = face drooping.

A = arms dropping by your sides, feeling very heavy.

S = slurred speech.

T = time to call 999

The Golden Hour

Let us reflect on the **GOLDEN HOUR**, which is the first hour from the appearance of the symptoms of **STROKE** (**F.A.S.T.**) or other Traumatic event, in which you have to reach a hospital with A&E services, for early diagnosis and professional treatment.

The following is a true story and is a prime example of the **GOLDEN HOUR** and being "in the right place at the right time".

Erik, a close family friend, had a stroke, on the same night as I had mine. Erik lives in Tallaght (a suburb in **DUBLIN**). He was taken to Tallafght hospital (30 mins away), was duly treated and then transferred to another specialist, stroke hospital. Like me, patralysis had set in. He received a "Lumbar puncture" administered by a Stroke specialist, a Chinese doctor. Erik, walked out of the hospital the following day. So, 1-Nil to Erik, and he is doing well.

Imagine how that outcome, made me feel in the early days of my stroke, and the myriad of questions, within me. So, I was right all along, there is or was a "silver bullet" out there, just like the Covid jab we have today. Now, I just have to accept my Fate, which I have done.

Post-it Notes

If your loved one lives alone, have these notes everywhere, on vanity and shaving mirrors, the fridge, toilet roll holder, bathroom door, anywhere that is visual, with the house area code on it. Get them an alarm necklace.

A tip for all: don't consume fizzy drinks in the evening or morning, before either physiotherapy or the arrival of visitors. With your exercises and moving about, you are most likely to fart and there is nowhere to hide and no one else to blame. We are all like seagulls who generally on lift-off shed their poo and gas, their motto being: an empty bowel is better than having a bad tenant. Humans are no different.

Cocooning

Get a craam from your local pharmacy: Sudocreme or Candelsine powder for groin rashes from sitting so much.

Venting

A healthy thing to do at when aimed at the nursing manager and doctor but not at your loved ones. It gets rid of all your toxic negative energy!

If you are experiencing **F.A.S.T**, take sharp intakes of breath, then exhale very slowly. This will prevent you from being overwhelmed.

Sleep Apnea

Most families, including mine, can be unaware that a family member may have this condition. They see it, but don't identify it as something that can be very serious and life-threatening for their loved one. The classic example is seeing an elderly family member snoozing and snoring on the sofa, head back, and no sound, after a big heavy meal as we all watch tv.

The danger is when the snoring stops and their breathing is very shallow. Wake them immediately. You should alert them and their loved ones to this condition, that they are totally unaware of. They can get help for it or die in silence. Lots of people pass away each year because of it.

OSAP - Obstructive Aleep Apnoea (OSA)

This is is quite common. It is a condition where the walls of the throat relax and narrow during sleep. This interrupts normal breathing.

It can lead to regular interrupted sleep. This can have a big impact on your quality of life. It increases the risk of developing certain conditions.

Apnoea

This is when the muscles and soft tissues in your throat relax and collapse. They do this enough to cause a total blockage of the airway. It's called an apnoea when your airflow is blocked for 10 seconds or more.

Hypopnoea

This is a partial blockage of the airway. It causes a reduction in your airflow of more than 50% for 10 seconds or more.

You can have more than 1 episode of apnoea and hypopnoea throughout the night. They can happen once every 1 or 2 minutes in severe cases.

Obstructive sleep apnoea (OSA) can usually be diagnosed by watching you sleeping. This can happen in a sleep clinic. It can also be done using a testing device worn overnight at home.

Talk to your GP if you think you have OSA. They may need to refer you to a sleep specialist for further tests and treatment.

Before talking to your GP, ask a partner, friend or relative to observe you while you're asleep. If you have OSA, they may be able to spot episodes of breathlessness.

Experiencing just 11 minutes of severe sleep apnoea – during which blood oxygen levels dip to below 90 per cent of normal – appears to roughly double the risk of death among men.

The disorder is caused by a collapse of the upper airway during sleep. Many of those who suffer from sleep apnoea are unaware of it and it is usually their bed partner who draws their attention to it. Symptoms include loud snoring, fatigue and sleepiness during the day.

"As well as health issues, sleep apnoea can cause a number of other problems, most notably marital disharmony," said Richard Hawksworth, a respiratory physiologist in Tallaght Hospital's sleep laboratory. "Research has also found sleep apnoea to be a factor in road deaths with drivers having fallen asleep at the wheel."

A range of overnight sleeping aids, such as the CPAP (continuous positive airway pressure) device, can help alleviate the condition. he Irish Sleep Apnoea Trust estimates that up to 12,000 people in the Republic have a severe version of the disorder, with some sufferers awakening more than 30 times an hour. Among those who have suffered from the condition is Taoiseach Brian Cowen.

The American Sleep Apnea Association estimates that 38,000 people in the United States die each year from heart disease with sleep apnea as a complicating factor. People with sleep apnea have difficulty breathing or stop breathing for short periods while sleeping. This treatable sleep disorder often goes undiagnosed.The Irish Nation lost one of its favourite rugby sons in **ANTHONY "AXEL" FOLEY** to sleep apnoea at the age of 40 in 2016, while in a Paris hotel, while overnighting before a big rugby game as coach to Munster. Anthony, had an underlying heart bcondition (arrythmia). People with Cardiac issues are susceptible to Sleep Apnea and its outcomes (dying in your sleep). If you notice a family member with the above symptoms, dont go lookin for info on Google, get the local doctor on board. Don't delay, do it today and help avoid **"A TRAGEDY for MANY"**.

A Special Thank You…

To Joan and her physio team, who did their very best to get me walking again but could not source any 1000 amp fuses anywhere. They're all 13 or10 amp nowadays. But they did train me to be very functional and cope with any challenges, in and out of the wheelchair and true to form I have not met any yet.

In the midst of all of this moving around, I was called upon to have my bowel cancer operation, a right Hemicolectomy. I was assigned to Professor Mark Regan at UHG. We met up and he introduced me to his team, plus Dr Cheraud (Ali Baba) Oliviva and Anna O'Mara, my flying angel, there when you need her.

After some discussion, he told me: "This will be microsurgery, with maybe a 2-inch incision into your gut. Dr Ali here will carry out the procedure, and there may be a very high risk of another stroke, given all your underlying conditions, namely, an enlarged left ventricle in your heart, arrhythmia and we need a haemotologist, whom we have on board, Ruth Gilmore at UHG."

I looked at Dr Ali Baba's hands and I swear he had fingers bigger than turnips and hands bigger than a shovel! No way will he get inside me, I thought and there and then the two of them decided that I would not be suitable for a Stoma, a bowel bag, with me being confined to a wheelchair. At the time, I did not understand the significance of their decision. However, my sister Maura, a nurse, who has to use a Stoma, informed me of my good fortune.

Dr Ali explained that he would place a plastic bag inside my bowel and remove the lymphatic tissue for analysis. As he brought me into theatre on the gurney, both of us were in deep conversation on the subject of climate pollution. I asked him, whose bag he was using, Tesco, Lidl, or Aldi? I got no reply. I warned him that my bag of tissue had better not be found washed up on some seashore somewhere! Dr Regan looked on, gobsmacked at Dr Ali and me having this banter as I was about to be anaesthetised.

Anyway, we all had a happy ending: no stroke, lymphatic tissue, all clear of cancer and I now smile at my wheelchair each day, feeling very grateful. A big thank you to Dr Regan and his team and Dr Maccon Keane and Dr Gilmore.

Today, as I added the above to my story, I found out to my great sadness that Anna O'Mara, one of the team, had passed away over a year ago. She was my angel in relation to my own operation. She would phone me each day in advance, to offer me reassurance, on any little thought or concern that might be niggling me.

Dearest Anna, may you rest in peace. I needed to speak to Anna again today as I am having another colonoscopy procedure in two days. Once again Anna's backup, Olivia was there to hold my hand and reassure me of what is in store for me on the day, as I will be in the hands of a different surgeon whom I have never met before. Like many, we are being assigned to others to catch up on cancer procedures, with many cancelled and hospitals closed due to the covid pandemic. I have no doubt that Anna will be there with me on the day and all the theatre staff involved.

Anna was only 51. R.I.P.

17

Back from The Brink

Great Relief all around with no second stroke occurring and once again I'm back from the brink!

Men

Have a regular 'manogram'; don't get clamped! Let's chat, let's talk.

Podcast: listen to "Where is my mind?" by Niall Breslin.

Your body also needs iron to make some hormones. As a result, iron deficiency anaemia may leave you tired and short of breath and aching muscles, post-exercise.

Your mind/brain will not function 100% without oxygen. Mind it.

Useful Services

1.   Your local, stroke, support group or health centre.

2.   www.flintfit.com and www.croi.ie www.ihf.ie

3.   www.remotion.co.uk Mollii suits or
        www.molllii.com

4.   Irish vacation tours. dave.gero@gmail.com

5.   Europe respite & rehab vacations. arranged

6.   Podcast by Niall Breslin "Where is my mind?"

Our happy loved ones, yippee! It's great to be back together again!

What could have been for me, could be for you. That's me. I hope you enjoyed it. Stay safe.

What's next? Crossing the line! We made it and achieved our goal, meeting our loved ones! Yippee! Well, that wasn't a life sentence in the care home, just a duration. Let's go back? I am knackered! Next? I need some respite after a journey like that; next? possibly? That's it, I'm done! More respite!

I strongly recommend, that everyone should book themselves into a Care-Home for a week of Respite care, just to have the experience, before the your own sudden inevitable 'curtain-call, beckons! So have an A&E bag ready and waiting. DONT FORGET to have your WILL drafted legally and witnessed in consideration for your Loved Ones, &for your own Peace of Mind!

Credits

Thank you to:

Dr Joe Curran

Steven & Sarah (my paramedics)

Keith Abbott

Karolina Robinson

Yvonne and Chloe at Merlin Park

The Physio Team at Merlin Park

Mike de Hoist and Noel at Merlin Park

Jessica O'Malley

Liam Bourke

Denise & Brendan

Nodlaig Keating

The Indian nation for all their healthcare angels

Dr Tom Walsh, Dr Robinson, Shaun O'Keefe and
Carol Goulding at University Hospital Galway

The Stiletto Team at University Hospital Galway

Janet Murphy and Filipinos and Co.

Steven and Sarah and all the Clonbur First Responders

Rachael Spillane and Cora

Marcin Usynnski (Super Mario)

Oliga Kobteva

Martina Greene, Tracy Egan, Carol Counsellor

Croi Stroke Support Group. Edel Bourke

Father Michael Twomey

SORIN

Ashford Castle

The Luskan Clan/Cong

Fintan Gorman/Cong

John Fergusson/Cong

Paddy Geraghty and Family

All the Hickey Clan at Buckeye

All the O'Driscoll Clan

The MS Society, Galway

Gerard Geraghty

David Frances & Gabriel & Eva Geraghty

Maura Francis

Sean Coyne, Coyne's Gastro, Connemara

Charlotte Barry

Anita & Peter & all at Connemara Resource Centre

Dr Mark Regan and Team

Ann Fahy and Co at Mowlam Healthcare

The 'Wisdomites' and my blessed mother, Mary

Yvonne, Alfie, Esme and Michael Hill

All of my Clonbur neighbours

Nigel Plummer

ALL STAFF AT MOWLAM, KILCOLGAN

Loyola

Fr. Diarmad & his Deaconites/Oranmore.

Adrianna, Aisling M. and Co at Mowlam Healthcare

All nurses and healthcare angels at Kilcolgan

Everyone at Kilcolgan Care Home, Galway

All at Centra, at Kilcolgan